C000088652

In the interest of creating a more extensive selection of rare historical book reprints, we have chosen to reproduce this title even though it may possibly have occasional imperfections such as missing and blurred pages, missing text, poor pictures, markings, dark backgrounds and other reproduction issues beyond our control. Because this work is culturally important, we have made it available as a part of our commitment to protecting, preserving and promoting the world's literature. Thank you for your understanding.

NORTH CORNWALL
FAIRIES AND LEGENDS

BY

ENYS TREGARTHEN

AUTHOR OF ' THE PISKEY-PURSE '

WITH INTRODUCTION BY HOWARD FOX, F.G.S.

Illustrated

NEW YORK
PUBLIC
LIBRARY

LONDON
WELLS GARDNER, DARTON & CO., LTD.
3, PATERNOSTER BUILDINGS, E.C.

THE NEW YORK
PUBLIC LIBRARY

2 0 16 /

ASTOR, LENOX AND
TILDEN FOUNDATIONS.

1906

NEW YORK
PUBLIC
LIBRARY

THE NEW YORK
PUBLIC LIBRARY

ASTOR, LENOX AND
TILDEN FOUNDATIONS.

Tintagel Castle.

C 398

T

Contents

	PAGE
INTRODUCTION	xi
THE ADVENTURES OF A PISKEY IN SEARCH OF HIS LAUGH	1
THE LEGEND OF THE PADSTOW DOOMBAR	51
THE LITTLE CAKE-BIRD	71
THE IMPOUNDED CROWS	99
THE PISKEYS' REVENGE	113
THE OLD SKY WOMAN	125
REEFY, REEFY RUM	131
THE LITTLE HORSES AND HORSEMEN OF PADSTOW	139
HOW JAN BREWER WAS PISKEY-LADEN	149
THE SMALL PEOPLE'S FAIR	159
THE PISKEYS WHO DID AUNT BETSY'S WORK	165
THE PISKEYS WHO CARRIED THEIR BEDS	177
THE FAIRY WHIRLWIND	183
NOTES	189

NEW YORK
PUBLIC
LIBRARY

List of Illustrations

	PAGE
TINTAGEL CASTLE · · · · *Frontispiece*	
KING ARTHUR'S CASTLE, LOOKING NORTH · ·	9
TINTAGEL CASTLE · · · · · ·	15
BY ROUGH TOR'S GRANITE-PILED HEIGHT THE BRIGHT LITTLE LANTERN WENT · · · · · ·	21
'NIGHT-RIDERS, NIGHT-RIDERS, PLEASE STOP!' · ·	37
'WHICH IS STILL CALLED KING ARTHUR'S SEAT' · ·	45
LIFEBOAT GOING OVER THE BAR OF DOOM · · ·	53
TRISTRAM BIRD COULD SEE OVER THE MAIDEN'S HEAD INTO THE POOL · · · · · · ·	55
TREBETHERICK BAY · · · · · ·	62
CHAPEL STILE · · · · · · ·	65
'IT IS THE MERMAID'S WRAITH,' CRIED AN OLD GRANFER MAN · · · · · · ·	67
TREGOSS MOOR · · · · · ·	73
ON THE WAY TO TAMSIN'S COTTAGE · · ·	75
'I HEAR THEM LAUGHING. LISTEN, GRANNIE!' · ·	83
THE ROCHE ROCKS · · · · ·	85
HE STEPPED ON TO PHILLIDA'S NOSE AS LIGHT AS THE FEATHERS OF THE OLD SKY WOMAN · · ·	91
'ALL THE CROWS IN THE PARISH CAME AS THEY WERE BIDDEN' · · · · · · ·	101
'PERHAPS YOU WOULD LIKE TO HEAR THE CROWS' VERSION OF THE TALE?' · · · · ·	105
THE PISKEYS GOT IN AND ATE UP THE BOWL OF JUNKET, AND PASSED OUT THE BISCUITS · · · ·	118

List of Illustrations

PAGE

'THE OLD SKY WOMAN SWEEPING OUT THE SKY GOOSE'S HOUSE' 128

SHE TOOK TO HER HEELS AND RAN FOR HER LIFE - - 135

SAW THEM STANDING ON THE TILE-RIDGE - - · 141

THEY GALLOPED MUCH FASTER THAN HE COULD RUN 145

RUINS OF CONSTANTINE CHURCH - - - - 153

THEY BEGAN TO DANCE ROUND HIM - - - - 157

NANNIE WENT ON THE MOORS AGAIN, AND TINKER FOLLOWED

HER - - - - - - - - 172

Introduction

THE tales contained in this little volume of North Cornwall fairy stories, by Enys Tregarthen, are either founded on folk-lore or they are folk-lore pure and simple.

The scene of the first story is laid amid the ancient walls and gateways of 'Grim Dundagel thron'd along the sea,' and other places not quite so well known by those who live beyond the Cornish land, but which, nevertheless, have a fascination of their own, especially Dozmare Pool, where Tregeagle's unhappy spirit worked at his hopeless task of emptying the pool with a crozan or limpet-shell 'that had a hole in it.'

This large inland lake, one mile in circumference, is of unusual interest, not only because of the Tregeagle legend that centres round Dozmare, but from a tradition, which many believe, that it was to this desolate moor, with its great tarn, that Sir Bedivere, King Arthur's faithful knight, brought the wounded King after the last great battle at Slaughter Bridge, on the banks of the Camel.

A wilder and more untamed spot could hardly be found even in Cornwall than Dozmare Pool and the

Introduction

barren moors surrounding it. As one stands by its dark waters, looking away towards the bare granite-crowned hills and listening to the wind sighing among the reeds and rushes and the coarse grass, one can realize to the full the weird legends connected with it, and one can see in imagination the huge figure of Tregeagle bending over the pool, dipping out the water with his poor little limpet-shell.

The Tregeagle legends are still believed in. When people go out to Dozmare Pool, they do not mention Tregeagle's name for fear that the Giant will suddenly appear and chase them over the moors!

On the golden spaces of St. Minver sand-hills the legends about this unearthly personage are not so easily realized, except on a dark winter's night, when the wind rages fiercely over the dunes and one hears a fearful sound, which the natives say is Tregeagle roaring because the sand-ropes that he made to bind his trusses of sand are all broken. St. Minver is not only known for its connection with the legend of Tregeagle, but it is one of the many parishes beloved by the Small People or Fairy Folk with whom Enys Tregarthen's little book has mostly to do.

Piskeys danced in their rings on many a cliff and common and moor in that delightful parish, and on other wild moors, commons and cliffs in many another parish in North and East Cornwall. Fairy horsemen, locally known as night-riders, used to steal horses from farmers' stables and ride them over the moors and commons till daybreak, when

Introduction

they left them to perish, or to find their way back to their stalls.

Numberless stories of the little Ancient People used to be told, which the cottagers often repeated to each other on winter evenings as they sat round the peat fires, and some of these Enys Tregarthen has retold. The author writes concerning them: 'Many of the legends were told me by very old people long since dead. The legend of the Doombar was told me when I was quite a small child by a very old person born late in the eighteenth century. The one of Giant Tregeagle came, I think, from the same source, but it is too far back to remember. I only know it was one of the stories of my childhood, as were also the Mole legend and some of the Piskey-tales, handed down from a dim past by our Cornish forebears.

'The legends about the Little People are very old, and some assert to-day that the tales about the Piskeys are tales of a Pigmy race who inhabited Cornwall in the Neolithic Period, and that they are answerable for most of the legends of our Cornish fairies. If this be so, the older stories are legends of the little Stone Men.

'The legends are numerous. Some of them are very fragmentary; but they are none the less interesting, for they not only give an insight into the world of the little Ancient People, but they also show how strongly the Cornish peasantry once believed in them, as perhaps they still do. For,

Introduction

strange as it may seem in these matter-of-fact days, there are people still living who not only hold that there are Piskeys, but say they have actually seen them! One old woman in particular told me not many months ago that she had seen "little bits of men in red jackets" on the moors where she once lived. She used to be told about the Piskeys when she was a child, and the old people of her day used to tell how "the little bits of men" crept in through the keyhole of moorland cottages when the children were asleep to order their dreams.'

These stories are given to the world in the hope that many besides children, for whom they are specially written, will find them interesting, and all lovers of folk-lore will be grateful to know that the iron horse and other modern inventions have not yet succeeded in driving away the Small People, nor in banishing the weird legends from our loved 'land of haunting charm.'

H. F.

The Adventures of a Piskey in
Search of his Laugh

'. . . A soft
Cradle of old tales.'
                    W. B. YEATS.

The Adventures of a Piskey in Search of his Laugh

HE moon was shining softly down on the grey ruins of King Arthur's Castle by the Tintagel sea, and on hundreds of little Piskeys dancing in a great Piskey-ring on the mainland, known as Castle Gardens.

In the centre of the ring stood a Little Fiddler, fiddling away with all his might, keeping time with his head and one tiny foot.

The faster he played and flung out the merry tune on the quiet moonlit night, the faster the Piskeys danced. As they danced they almost burst their sides with laughter, and their laughter and the music of the Little Fiddler was distinctly heard by an old man and his wife, who then lived in the cottage near the castle.

North Cornwall Fairies

One little Piskey, somewhat taller than a clothes-peg, was the best dancer there, and his laugh was the merriest. He was dancing with a Piskey about his own size, who could hardly keep step with his twinkling feet.

As the Piskeys careered round and round the Piskey-ring, the tiny chap who was the best dancer, and had the merriest laugh, suddenly stopped laughing, and his little dancing feet gave under him, and down he went with a crash, dragging his little companion with him. Before they could pick themselves up, the Piskeys who were coming on behind, not seeing the two sprawling on the ring, fell on them, and in another moment Little Fiddler Piskey saw a moving heap of green-coated little bodies and a brown tangle of tiny hands and feet.

So amazed was he at such an unusual sight that he stopped fiddling, and let his fiddle slip out of his hand unnoticed on the grass.

When the Little Men had picked themselves up, except the one who had caused the mishap, they began to pitch into him for tumbling and causing them to tumble, when something in his tiny face made them stop.

'What made you go down on your stumjacket like that when you were dancing so beautifully?' asked a Piskey not unkindly.

'I don't know,' he answered, looking up at his little brother Piskey with a strange expression in his face, which was pinched and drawn, and pale as one

Piskey in Search of his Laugh

of their own Piskey-stools; and instead of a laugh in his dark little eyes there was misery and woe.

The strange expression in his eyes quite frightened the Piskeys, and one said: 'What is the matter with you? You are looking worse than a cat in a fit.'

'Am I?' said the poor little Piskey. 'I am feeling very queer. It was a queerness that made me fall on my little stumjacket. Am I ill like those great men and women creatures we sometimes entice into the bogs with Piskey-lights?'

'We have never heard of a Piskey getting ill or sick,' said a little brown Piskey, 'have we?' turning to speak to the Little Fiddler, who had come over to his companions, bringing his fiddle with him.

'I most certainly haven't,' answered the Little Fiddler.

'Then what is the matter with me, if I'm not sick?' asked the little Piskey who was looking so queer.

'Perhaps Granfer Piskey will be able to tell you, for I can't,' said the Tiny Fiddler.

'Where is Granfer Piskey?' asked the poor little sufferer. 'I am afraid I am getting worse, for all the dance has left my legs.'

'Granfer Piskey is over on the Island,' cried a little Piskey.

'So he is,' said all the other Piskeys, sending their glance in that direction, where, on the edge of a beetling cliff facing Castle Gardens, stood a tiny old man, with a white beard flowing down to his bare little feet. He was dressed, as were all the other Piskeys, in a bright green coat and a red stocking cap.

He disappeared into a Piskey-hole the Piskeys had dug in the cliff, which led down into an underground passage between the Island and the mainland, and very soon he reappeared from another hole in Castle Gardens, a few feet from where the little Piskeys were anxiously awaiting him.

' Why are you not fiddling, dancing and laughing ?' asked the little Whitebeard, winking his eyes on the silent little Piskey crowd, standing near their little brother Piskey who was looking so queer. ' You are wasting precious time standing here doing nothing. Before a great while the moon will have set over Trevose, and the time for merry-making and high-jinks will be over,' he added, as not a Piskey spoke.

' We are not fiddling, dancing and laughing because of something that has befallen our little brother,' said the Tiny Fiddler at last, pointing to the poor little Piskey who had raised himself to a sitting position and was seated on the Piskey-ring.

' He is a rum-looking little customer, sure 'nough,' said the old Whitebeard, glancing in the direction of the place where the Little Fiddler pointed. ' What is the matter with him ?'

' That is what we want to know,' answered the

Piskey in Search of his Laugh

Little Fiddler. 'Come and have a closer look at him, Granfer Piskey;' and Granfer Piskey came.

'What is the matter with him?' asked one of the Piskeys when the Whitebeard had stared down a minute or more on the little atom of misery sitting humped up on the edge of the great green ring like a toad on a hot shovel. 'You are so old and wise, you will be able to tell us what ails him, if anybody can. He thinks he is sick like the big people we lead a fine dance round the fields and commons some-times,' as Granfer Piskey stood stock-still before the little afflicted Piskey, winking and blinking and solemnly shaking his head.

'He is not sick like those people of whom you spoke,' said the Whitebeard at last. 'He has——'

'The make-outs,' shrilled a little voice with a laugh somewhere in the background.

'No, he hasn't the make-outs, you impudent little rascal!' said Granfer Piskey, without lifting his gaze from the poor little fellow on the edge of the ring. 'That's a complaint from which you apparently suffer.'

'What has he?' asked the Tiny Fiddler, im-patiently scraping his fiddle-stick over his fiddle, as if to emphasize his words.

'It isn't what he has, but what he *hasn't*,' said the old Whitebeard, in the same slow, solemn voice. 'I was going to say that our poor little brother has lost his laugh.'

'Lost his laugh!' cried little Fiddler Piskey and all

the other little Piskeys ; and their tiny faces of consternation showed what a terrible thing had befallen their poor little brother.

'Yes, he has had the sad misfortune to lose his laugh,' said the little old Whitebeard, winking and blinking harder than ever as he stood before the unhappy little Piskey who had lost his laugh; 'and, worse still, he is quite done for till he finds it again.'

'Where has my laugh gone to, Granfer Piskey?' asked the miserable little Piskey who had met with that dreadful misfortune.

'I don't know more than the Little Man in the moon,' answered the tiny old Whitebeard; 'but if I were you I would go and look for it.'

'Where must I go and look for my laugh?' asked the poor little Piskey.

'I have not the smallest idea; but I should go and search for it till I found it.'

'Will you come with me and search for my laugh?' asked the little Piskey, with a look of anxiety in his wee dark eyes, as Granfer Piskey was moving away.

'I am afraid I can't. It is my duty to stop with your brothers to see that they don't grow silly and lose their laugh. Besides, it is not quite the thing for an old Whitebeard like me to go travelling about the country with a youngster like you, in search of a laugh.'

'Will you go with me to look for my laugh?' asked the little Piskey, fixing his gaze on the Tiny Fiddler.

'I would go with you gladly, if I were not Fiddler

Piskey in Search of his Laugh

Piskey,' he answered, touching his fiddle lightly
with his bow. ' But if I were to go gallivanting up
and down the country in search of your laugh, there
would be nobody to play the dancing tune when our
brothers dance in the moonshine.'

King Arthur's Castle, looking North.

' Won't one of you go with me and help me to
find my laugh ?' begged the miserable little fellow,
glancing from one Piskey to another as they crowded
round him.

' We would if we hadn't so much dancing to do,
they said. ' We have to dance in every Piskey-ring

from Tintagel Head to Crackington Hawn up St. Gennys, before the moon grows as small as a wren's claw.'

'Must I go by myself to search for my laugh?' said the poor little Piskey in a heart-breaking voice.

'Yes, you must go by yourself to look for your laugh,' answered all the little Piskeys. 'You should not have been so foolish as to lose it;' and the selfish little Brown Men—Granfer Piskey, Fiddler Piskey, and all the other Piskeys—turned their backs on their unfortunate little brother, and ran away across the gardens and over the cliffs towards Bossiney, half-way between which was another big Piskey-ring; and by-and-by the poor little Piskey who had lost his laugh heard in the distance, as he sat all alone in the great grassy place, their merry laughter and the music of Fiddler Piskey's tiny fiddle.

He was a very sad little Piskey as he listened to the merriment of his little brother Piskeys, and the moon, sailing along the dark velvety blue of the midnight sky above the ruins of King Arthur's Castle and Gardens, never looked down on such a woe-begone little Piskey before. He had always been happy and gay till now, and having no laugh was such a strange experience that it was no wonder he felt as miserable and wisht * as he did.

As he sat there all alone on the ring his own little dancing feet had helped to make, two tiny hands were suddenly thrust up out of a small earth-heap

* Sad.

half a foot from where he was sitting. So dainty were the hands, that he thought they belonged to one of the little Good People, a distant relation of his; and thinking that somehow one had got buried under the earth, he got up from the ring to help her out, and, without waiting to say 'Allow me,' or anything so polite, he caught hold of the wee hands, and pulling with all his strength, he dragged something very dark and soft out of the earth-heap, and saw to his surprise and disgust that it was the round plump body of a mole!

'Whatever did you drag me out of the want-hill for, you horrid creature! whoever you are?' cried the mole, who was not as soft as she looked. 'It took me hours to throw up that beautiful hill, and now it has fallen down into my tunnel, and my work will all have to be done over again, thanks to you.'

'I am so sorry,' said the Piskey. 'I saw two dinky little hands sticking up, and thought a relation of mine had got buried; and when I did my best to get her out I found it was only a *want*, as the country people call you moles.'

'A want indeed!' exclaimed the mole. 'Who are you, pray, to speak so disdainfully? If I am only a want, I was not always the poor thing I am now. Once upon a time I was a very great lady, and because I was foolish and proud and very vain of my beauty I was turned into a mole. My little hands are the only things left of me to show who I once was.'

'I am very sorry for you,' said the Piskey, with

strong note of sympathy in his voice, so entirely new to him that he scarcely knew it was himself speaking; for Piskeys, although they are merry and gay, are often selfish in the extreme. ' I am more sorry for you than I can say,' he went on. ' It cannot be nice to be only a want, when once you were a beautiful lady. I am a Piskey,' as the little dark mole was silent.

' A Piskey, are you ?' she cried, speaking at last. ' I remember you little Piskey people quite well, and have cause to remember. Once, when I was a grand lady and wore fine clothes, you Piskeys led me into a bog and spoilt my silken gown. I did not bless you then, and I do not bless you now. You are still up to your tricks, I find to my cost, for you have done your best to pull down my house about my ears.'

' I did not mean to do anything so unkind,' said the little Piskey. ' I am not merry enough now to play games on anyone.'

' How is that ?' asked the mole.

' I have lost my laugh, and my heart is as heavy as lead,' he answered sorrowfully.

' Lost your laugh !' cried the mole. ' That is very strange.'

' Yes, it is; and I am quite done for, so Granfer Piskey told my little brothers, till I find it again.'

' Why don't you go and look for your laugh instead of throwing down want-hills?' said the mole severely. ' It would be more to your credit if you did.'

Piskey in Search of his Laugh

'I suppose it would,' replied the Piskey; 'but, unfortunately, I don't know where to go and look for my laugh. Have you seen it?'

'No, I haven't,' snapped the mole; 'I can't see without eyes. I have lost my eyesight through working underground for so many long centuries.'

'Do you know anybody who has seen my laugh?' asked the little Piskey, 'and who would kindly tell me where to go and find it?'

'I am afraid I don't,' answered the mole, 'except the Little Man in the Lantern. He is the most likely person I know to have seen your laugh. He is always flipping about the country in the night-time in his little Lantern, and sees most things that wander by night. He is a kind-hearted little fellow, and if he has seen your laugh, he'll be sure to help you to find it. You know, of course, where the little Lantern Man is to be found?'

'I have seen his Lantern in the marshes sometimes.' answered the Piskey. 'I saw it rush by a few weeks ago, when I and my brothers were lying snug and warm in a great Piskey-bed at Rough Tor Marsh. But as I do not happen to know the Lantern Man, will you please come with me to Rough Tor Marsh and ask him if he has seen my laugh?'

'What next will you ask me to do?' cried the mole. 'No, I cannot go with you. I am far too busy to go tramping round the country with a little Brown Piskey like you, in search of a laugh. I have a tunnel to make across Castle Gardens for my dear

little baby wants to run about in, and I must do it
before the sun shines over the Tors. If you really
want to find your laugh, you must go and ask the
Lantern Man yourself. The sooner you go the
better, or you may lose the chance of asking him if
he has seen it.'

' I dare say you are right,' said the little Piskey,
with a heavy sigh. ' But I don't like the idea of
travelling all the way from here to Rough Tor
Marsh. My feet are heavy like my heart, now I have
lost my laugh; yet I suppose I must go, for I am a
wisht poor thing without it, and you would say so,
too, Mrs. Mole, if your eyesight wasn't so bad.'

' Mrs. Mole, indeed !' snapped the velvet-coated
little creature, raising her tiny hands in anger at
such an insult. ' I beg to tell you that I am *not* Mrs.
Mole, but the Lady Want, and that, although I have
fallen from my high estate, I am still a lady of high
degree, as my tiny hands bear witness;' and she
held them out for him to see.

' I'm not up in fine distinctions,' said the little
Piskey in a humble voice, ' and I beg your ladyship's
pardon.'

The Piskey's sad little voice so appeased ' the Lady
Want ' that she fully forgave his ignorance, and told
him he was quite nice-mannered for a Piskey, and
hoped the little Lantern Man had seen his laugh,
and would be able to tell him where to find it ; and
then her little ladyship disappeared into the mole-
hill, her tiny lady hands and all !

Piskey in Search of his Laugh

When she had gone, the little Piskey turned his face towards the east, where the Tors rose up dark and shadowy against the moonlit sky. Then he looked back at the great keep, and turned his glance on the Castle Gardens, where, in the long ago, courtly knights and great ladies walked among the

Tintagel Castle.

flowers that blossomed there under the shadow of the loopholed walls, and listened, as they walked, to the music of the Tintagel sea and the great waves that sometimes broke against the dark cliffs of the headland on which the grim old castle stood, where Good King Arthur was born.

The little Piskey was saying good-bye to that

delightful spot, with its soft turf and the beautiful Piskey-ring on which he had danced times without number; for the poor, lonely little fellow did not know if he should ever come back again. Then he broke off a bit of a knapweed stem for a staff to help him on his journey to Rough Tor Marsh,* and before the moon had laid down a lane of silver fire on the rippling waters between Tintagel Head and Trevose, the little Piskey had set out on his travels in search of his laugh.

Piskeys always travel by night, and after many nights of wandering, the little Piskey who had lost his laugh came to the bog country, where he had last seen the little Lantern.

Very tired and footsore was that poor little Piskey after his long journey, for, having lost his laugh, he had no dance in his feet to help him along, and he felt so done up as he sat by the great bog, or Piskey-bed, as he called it, that he did not much care whether he found his laugh or not. But when he had rested awhile he felt better, and looked over the great marshy place with eager eyes, to see if the little Lantern Man was anywhere about. To his delight he was; for far away in the distance he saw the white gleam of his Lantern.

He kept his eyes upon the light, and by-and-by, when the Lantern came rocking over the bog in his direction, he stood up on the edge of the water ready to call. It disappeared ever so many times among

* A bog near Rough Tor.

the bog-myrtles and willows, but every time it reappeared it was closer. When it came near enough
for him to see the little Lantern Man inside, he
shouted :

'Little Man in the Lantern, please stop: I want
to ask you something.' But whether the Lantern
Man heard or not, he did not stop, and he and his
Lantern flipped by the disappointed little Piskey as
quickly as a widdy-mouse * on the wing, and was
lost to sight in the reeds and rushes on the other
side of the great marsh.

After a while the little Lantern Man came back to
the place where the Piskey was still standing, and
the light from the Lantern was brighter and softer
than a hedge full of glow-worm lights shining all at
once.

As the Lantern was passing the little Piskey, he
called out louder than before, 'Little Man in the
Lantern, please stop ; I want to ask you something.'
But the little Lantern Man did not stop, and he and
his Lantern rushed by as quickly as before, and the
poor little Piskey followed the rocking Lantern with
his eyes over the great marsh.

Just as he was in despair of the wonderful little
Lantern coming his way again, it came, and so fast
did it come, and so afraid was he of its passing him
without making himself heard, that he shouted with
all his might, 'Please, little Lantern Man, stop; I
want to ask you something.' And to his joy the little

* A bat.

Lantern Man stopped. The door of the little Lantern opened wide, and a tiny, shining face looked out.

'Did anybody call?' asked the little Lantern Man in a voice so kind that the Piskey's little heart leaped for joy.

'Yes, I called,' said the little Piskey. 'I called twice before, but you did not stop.'

'I never heard you call till now,' said the little Lantern Man. 'Who are you, and what do you want?'

'I am an unfortunate little Piskey who has lost his laugh,' answered the Piskey, 'and I have tramped all the way from Tintagel Head to Rough Tor Marsh to ask if you have seen it.'

'Lost your laugh, you poor little chap!' ejaculated the little Lantern Man in the same kind voice. 'How came you to lose it?'

The little Piskey told him how he had lost his laugh, and what Granfer Piskey had said, and how the mole who called herself the Lady Want had told him to come to him.

'I would gladly help you to find your laugh if I knew where it was,' said the Lantern Man when the Piskey had told him all; 'but, unfortunately, I have never seen it.'

'Haven't you?' cried the poor little Piskey. 'I *am* disappointed. As you are always travelling about the country in your little Lantern, I felt sure you had seen my laugh.'

Piskey in Search of his Laugh

'I only travel in marshy ground,' said the little Lantern Man, still standing in the doorway of his tiny Lantern; 'and your laugh may not have passed along my way.'

'Do you happen to know anybody else who has seen my laugh?' asked the little Piskey anxiously.

'Nobody except Giant Tregeagle, of whom I dare say you have heard—that unhappy fellow who for some terrible wrong-doing has to dip Dozmare* Pool dry with a limpet-shell.'

'Yes, I have heard about that great Giant from Granfer Piskey,' answered the little Piskey. 'He was a wicked seigneur who once had a fine house at Dozmare Pool and a great park on Bodmin Moors, and he is often flying about the country with the Wicked One at his heels.'

'The very same,' cried the little Lantern Man. 'He travels from east to west, and from west to south, and back again. He will be sure to have seen your laugh.'

'I am afraid my laugh is too small for a great big giant to have noticed, even if it passed him,' said the little Piskey.

'He isn't so big but what he can see a laugh,' said the little Lantern Man. 'You had better go and ask him.'

'I don't know where he is,' said the little Piskey, who was in a most dejected frame of mind.

* Pronounced Dozmary.

'He is at Dozmare Pool—or was not long since, doing his best to dip the big pool dry.'

'I am rather tired after tramping here from Tintagel,' said the little fellow, 'and I don't feel like going all the way to Dozmare Pool. I have no spring in my legs since my laugh left me,' he added, as the little Lantern Man smiled rather sadly. 'I never knew what it was to be tired and wisht before I lost my laugh.'

'I don't suppose you did, you poor little chap!' cried the little Lantern Man, 'and you must do all you can to find your laugh. I am going to Dozmare Pool, or the Magic Lake, as it was called in the long ago ; and if you don't mind travelling in my Lantern, I'll give you a lift as far as that.'

'Will you?' exclaimed the little Piskey, his tiny brown face brightening as the Lantern Man smiled. 'You are very kind, and I will go with you gladly.'

'That's right!' cried the little Lantern Man ; and he held out his hand, which shone like his face, and helped the little brown Piskey into his Lantern.

When the Piskey was safe inside the Lantern, he thought it was the very brightest place he was ever in—'even brighter than a fairy's palace,' he said.

'There is no seat in my Lantern except the floor,' said the little Lantern Man, as the Piskey looked about him. 'The floor is not uncomfortable, if you care to sit down. I always sleep on it when my night work of giving light to the poor things that live in the marshes is done.'

Piskey in Search of his Laugh

'I would rather stand, thank you,' returned the Piskey. 'I can look out of your windows better.'

'Do as you like, only it is my duty to tell you that you would be safer on the floor. My Lantern and

By Rough Tor's granite-piled height the bright little Lantern went.

I travel so fast that the creatures that fly by night often knock up against us and turn us upside down.'

The little Lantern Man shut the door of his Lantern as he was speaking, and in another minute they were rushing over Rough Tor Marsh at a fearful speed, and the little Piskey had to hold on to the frame of one of the tiny windows to keep himself on his feet. By Rough Tor's granite-piled heights the bright little Lantern went. On by Bronwilli (Brown Willy) it sped, and by many a solitary hill, almost as wild and untamed as old Rough Tor itself. Over lonely moors, bogs, rivers, and streams, it flew, and rocked and whirled as it went. As it sped on it bumped against all manner of strange creatures, and once a night-hawk * turned the little Lantern upside down, and the Piskey found himself standing on his head with his tiny lean legs sticking up in the air ; and he looked so funny that the little Lantern Man laughed till the tears ran down his shining face, and if the Piskey had had his laugh he would have laughed too!

On and on the Lantern rushed, zigzagging up and down, down and up, and as it went strange moths and queer things that go about only by night fluttered their wings against its bright windows and door. Once a widdy-mouse, with a face like a cat, looked in, and then vanished into the darkness ; and once a short-eared owl gripped the Lantern in his talons, but it sped on all the same.

About an hour after midnight the Lantern reached Dozmare Pool, which lies on the top of a great lonely moor surrounded by desolate hills. The moon was only a few days old, and had set long before the sun had gone down ; but it was by no means dark by the big pool, for there was starshine from

* Nightjar.

innumerable stars, and also the light that fell from the wonderful little Lantern.

The little Lantern Man stopped his Lantern on a boulder by the pool, where was stretched a huge dark form, almost as big as a headland. It was Giant Tregeagle, lying face down on the margin of the pool, dipping water with a limpet-shell which had a hole in it.

The little Lantern Man opened the door of his Lantern, and telling the little Piskey that now was his chance to ask the Giant about his laugh, he helped him out.

'Shout into his ear till he hears you,' he whispered, hanging out of his door, 'and don't despair if he does not hear you just at first.'

The Piskey stepped up quite close to the great Giant, and he looked so tiny beside him that the little Lantern Man laughed, and said he was like a God's little cow* by the side of a plough-horse. 'Why,' he said, 'his ear alone would make a dozen little chaps like you and me. Now I must be off and give light to the poor things that want light. Good luck to you, my friend, in finding your laugh;' and the little Lantern Man closed the door of his Lantern, which sped away over the big pool, shedding light as it went.

The Piskey watched the Lantern till it was hidden among the reeds and rushes, and then he turned his face to the Giant's ear, and when he had climbed up into it, he shouted:

* The ladybird.

'Giant Tregeagle, Giant Tregeagle, I am a poor little Piskey who has lost his laugh. Please stop dipping water for a minute, and tell me if you have seen it.'

But the Giant took no notice of the little Piskey, and went on dipping out water with a limpet-shell that had a hole in it.

Again and again the tiny brown Piskey shouted into the Giant's ear, but the big Giant took no more notice of his little piping voice than if a fly had buzzed close to his ear, and went on dipping.

Once more the Piskey shouted with all the voice he had, thrusting his red-capped head into the hollow of the Giant's ear as he shouted:

'Giant Tregeagle, Giant Tregeagle, I am a poor little Piskey who has lost his laugh. Please stop dipping water for a minute, and tell me if you have seen it.'

This time the Giant heard, and without pausing for a moment his hopeless task of emptying the pool dry, he said:

'What tiny squeak did I hear?'

The Piskey was too frightened to answer, for Giant Tregeagle's voice was almost as loud as the roar of breakers breaking in the cavern under King Arthur's Castle, and the tiny fellow crouched down in the curl of the Giant's ear.

'What tiny squeak did I hear?' again asked the Giant; and the little Piskey, taking his courage in both his hands, answered back as loud as he could:

Piskey in Search of his Laugh

'It was a little Piskey who spoke to you—a little Piskey who has had the great misfortune to lose his laugh.'

'A little Piskey has lost his laugh, has he?' roared Giant Tregeagle. 'Why, that's nothing compared to a Giant who has lost his soul!'

'Have you lost your soul?' cried the little Piskey, who, having got the Giant's ear, could now make his tiny voice distinctly heard.

'Yes, I have lost my soul,' moaned the great fellow, and his moan shivered over the surface of Dozmare Pool, and made all the sallows that grew beside it shiver and shake as if a blasting wind had passed over them; and the reeds and rushes growing in the water sighed so sadly that the little Piskey felt ever so wisht, and sighed too.

'How did you come to lose your soul, Mister Giant?' asked the little Piskey after a while.

'That's a question,' answered the Giant, beginning again his hopeless task of emptying the pool.

'Have you never looked for your soul?' queried the tiny fellow who, having lost his laugh, felt very sorry for the unhappy Giant who had lost so precious a thing as his soul.

'It was no good to look for my soul when I gave it away in exchange for wealth,' cried the Giant; 'I can never get it back again unless I empty this big pool of every drop of water that is in it.'

'And can't you do that, and you a giant?' asked the little Piskey in surprise.

North Cornwall Fairies

'I am afraid I can't with a limpet-shell that has a hole in it; and I am not allowed to use any other.'

'Will you let me help you to empty the pool?' asked the tiny Piskey. 'I am only a little bit of a chap compared with you, I know—a God's little cow by the side of a plough-horse, the Man in the Lantern said,' as the Giant laughed sardonically; 'and my dinky hand is nothing for size, but it hasn't a hole in it.'

'You can help me if you like,' said the Giant with another sardonic laugh. 'It will be perhaps another case of a mouse freeing the lion!'

'Who knows?' cried the Piskey, who took the Giant's remark quite seriously; and climbing out of the huge ear, he slid down over the boulder to the pool, and making a dipper of his tiny hand, began to dip out water as fast as he could, and never stopped dipping once till a movement behind him made him pause, and, looking up, he saw the great big Giant on his feet towering above him like a tor, with an awful look of rage on his face.

'I can never, never, empty Dozmare Pool with a limpet-shell that has a hole in it,' howled the Giant—'no, not if I dip till the Day of Doom;' and he flung the shell into the big pool. As he flung it a great blast of rage broke from him and lashed the dark water of the big pool in fury. He howled and howled, and his howls were heard in every part of the lonely waste surrounding the pool, and went roaring round and round the far-stretching moors, and were echoed by the desolate hills. By-and-by the Giant turned his back on the pool and strode away in the direction of the sea, howling and roaring as he went.

The little Piskey was so terrified by the Giant's roaring that he crept into a water-rat's hole, and never ventured out for a night and a day.

The second night after the Giant had gone he came out of the hole to see if he had returned, but he had not. He was disappointed in spite of the fright he had received, for the Giant had never told him whether he had seen his laugh, and he did not know where to go in search of it, or whom to ask if it had been seen.

As he thought about this, he became very miserable—almost as miserable as the unhappy Giant who had sold his soul, and he wished with all his heart that the kind little Man in the Lantern would come his way again. As he was wishing this he looked over the big pool, which was very dark and unlit by single star, when something very soft and bright smote the black water on the opposite side of the pool.

Thinking it was the dear little Man in his Lantern come in answer to his wish, he fixed his gaze upon the brightness, and in a minute or two a little Barge shot out from the reeds and came swiftly towards him, and he saw (for the Piskeys can see in the dark like a cat) that the Barge was being rowed across the big pool by a little old man. The soft light that smote the water came from the prow of the little craft and lit up the face of the Bargeman, which

was half turned towards the Piskey, and was very
seared and brown.

When the Barge came near the spot where the
Piskey was standing, the Tiny Bargeman said:

'Who are you, looking as if you had the world on
your back? and what are you doing here this time of
night, when all good folk ought to be in bed?'

'I am a poor unfortunate Piskey who has lost his
laugh,' answered the tiny little Piskey, and his voice
was very sad.

'It is a dreadful thing to lose your laugh,' said
the little old Bargeman.

'It is,' responded the little Piskey. 'The little
Man in the Lantern thought so too, and he brought
me all the way from Rough Tor Marsh to Dozmare
Pool in his Lantern to ask Giant Tregeagle if he
had seen it.'

'And didn't you ask Giant Tregeagle that important question after the little Lantern Man had
brought you so far?' asked the little Bargeman.

'I did, but he was so troubled about something he
had lost—his soul it was—that he forgot to say
whether he had seen my laugh.'

'That is a pity, for the Giant is now on St. Minver
sand-hills making trusses of sand and sand-ropes to
bind them with, and when the sand-ropes break in
his hand—which they are sure to do when he tries
to lift them—he will fly away to Loe Bar* to work
at another impossible task.'

* Near Helston.

Piskey in Search of his Laugh

' How do you know that ?' asked the little Piskey.

The Tiny Bargemen looked at the green-coated, red-capped little Piskey with a strange expression in his dark eyes for a second or two, and then he said :

' I have lived so long in the world that I know most things. People who knew me in a far-away time called me Merlin the Magician, and said I had all the secrets of the world in the back of my head.'

' Then you will be able to tell me where my laugh has gone to ?' struck in the little Piskey eagerly.

' I was speaking more of the past than of the present,' said the Tiny Bargeman. ' Since the time of which I spoke, I have lived here by this lake, now called Dozmare Pool. I lived sealed up in a stone, into which the Lady of the Lake shut me till a hundred years or so ago.'

' How very unkind of the Lady to put you into a stone !' said the little Piskey indignantly. ' Whatever did she do it for ?'

' Thereby hangs a tale which is not good for a small Piskey like you to hear,' returned the Tiny Bargeman, with another strange look in his dark, mysterious little eyes. ' When Nimue, the Lady of the Lake, shut me up in the stone—like a toad in a hole she said—she thought she had done for me, and that I should soon die. But Merlin, the man who worked magic, was not so easily got rid of.'

' And didn't you die ?' asked the Piskey innocently.

' You must have lost your wits, as well as your

laugh, to ask such a stupid question,' said the Tiny Bargeman. ' I did not die, or I should not be sitting in this Barge now. But I grew down to the tiny old fellow you now see me through working my way out of that dreadful stone. My magical powers have also dwindled, I fear; for they are as nothing to what they once were. Therefore I am no longer Merlin the Magician, but only Merlin the Bargeman of Dozmare Pool.'

' And can't you tell me where my laugh is ?' asked the little Piskey wistfully. ' I am a miserable, poor thing without my laugh.'

' I'm sure you are,' said the Tiny Bargeman, ' and I'll do what I can to help you to find it. I wasn't shut up in a stone all those centuries for nothing, as, perhaps, you have not lost your laugh for nothing. I'll tell you at once that your laugh has never been near this desolate spot, but it is possible that Giant Tregeagle may have seen it on his wild flight down to St. Minver sand-hills, or maybe he has seen it on the golden dunes. I advise you to go there and ask him.'

' How can I get to the sand-hills ?' asked the poor little Piskey. ' It would take me such a long time to get there with no dance in my feet; and there is no little Lantern Man here to give me a lift in his Lantern.'

' You need not trouble your head how you are to get to the sand-hills. I'll take you near there in my Barge.'

Piskey in Search of his Laugh

' In your Barge?' echoed the little Piskey, looking over his shoulder to the long stretch of country between him and the sea, and then at the great pool set like a cup on the top of the moors, with no visible outlet.

' You are wondering how I can take you to the great outer sea,' said the Tiny Bargeman. ' For your satisfaction I will tell you that there is an underground waterway that leads down to Trebetherick Bay, close to St. Minver sand-hills. I will take you there in my Barge.'

' Why are you so kind?' asked the little Piskey, looking gratefully at the little old Bargeman. ' My brothers were not nearly so kind.'

' I saw you helping the wicked Giant to dip this great mere dry, and I thought so kind a deed deserved another,' answered the Little Bargeman lightly ; ' and I told myself as I watched you that I would do you a kindness, if you needed a kindness. Will you let me take you to Trebetherick Bay ?'

' Gladly,' answered the little Piskey.

' Get into my Barge, then,' cried the little old Bargeman ; and the Piskey scrambled in and sat in the stern of the Barge facing the Bargeman.

' I like rowing about this pool,' remarked the Tiny Bargeman, as he put his little craft about and began to row from the shore. ' It has so many memories. It was here by this mere that the Lady of the Lake (not the one who shut me up in a stone) forged the wonderful Excalibur, the two-handled sword with the jewelled hilt, which she gave to Arthur the King, who, you know, afterwards ruled all the land. It was here that Sir Bedivere—one of the Knights of the far-famed Round Table—flung the sword by order of the wounded King, and was caught by the Lake Lady's uplifted arm. It was here—— But you are not listening,' he cried, breaking off his sentence as he noticed that the little Piskey was not paying any attention to what he was saying.

' I'm afraid I wasn't,' he said, very much ashamed. ' I am very dull and stupid since I lost my laugh.'

' You can't be more stupid than I was when I was shut up in the stone,' said the tiny old Bargeman ; ' and I can well excuse your stupidity.'

He said nothing more, for just then the Barge reached the shore from which it had put off, and, without getting out, he reached over and touched a big stone with an oar. He had no sooner touched the stone than it sprang back, and revealed a dark, deep tunnel, into which the little Barge shot like a thing alive.

' This underground waterway was known to the fair ladies who lived by the pool, and who took away the wounded King in their little ship to the Vale of Avilion,' remarked the Bargeman when the stone shut up itself behind them.

' Did they ?' asked the little Piskey, trying to look interested.

' Yes,' he answered ; ' and they also knew of another waterway, which will never be revealed to anybody except by the Good King,' he added half to himself, looking straight before him into the darkness of the narrow passage as he steered.

The tiny Barge, which was a very ancient-looking little craft, with a gilded dragon forming its prow, sped on. But for its size, it might well have been the same little ship to which Merlin, the little old Bargeman, had just referred. The waterway was very long and deep, and the water ran so swiftly that the Barge did not now require to be rowed. It was also very dark, and the only light that shone was the light from the little boat.

The little old Bargeman did not speak again till a roaring fell on their ears.

'It is the noise of water breaking on Padstow Doombar,' he said, as the little Piskey looked frightened.

'I thought it was Giant Tregeagle howling,' gasped the little Piskey.

'He hasn't tried to lift his sand-ropes yet, and he won't begin his howl of rage till he finds how brittle they are,' said the Little Bargeman. 'And a very good thing for you,' he added; 'for he will be far too angry to tell you whether he has seen your laugh when the ropes of sand break in his great hand. There! we are close now to the great outer sea,' he cried, as the thunder of waves broke more loudly on their ears, and they saw the light of many stars through a narrow opening; and the next minute the little Barge came out into Trebetherick Bay.

'You only have to go up across the hillocks,' said the little old Bargeman, helping the little Piskey out of the barge, 'and if you follow your nose you will soon get to where the Giant is busy making sand-ropes.'

'Thank you for bringing me,' said the little Piskey; but he never knew whether he was heard or not, for the Tiny Bargeman and his ancient Barge vanished as he spoke.

The Piskey made haste to follow his nose, and he scrambled up a sand-bank, and hastened as fast as his feet could take him over the sandy common, till he came to the place where Giant Tregeagle was sitting making sand-ropes to bind his trusses of sand which lay all around him. He was sitting by a hillock, his great head showing just above it, when the Piskey came near.

The little Piskey climbed nearly to the top of the hillock, and when he got close to the Giant's ear he shouted:

'I am the little Piskey who told you he had lost his laugh. Please stop making sand-ropes for a minute and tell me if you have seen it.'

But the big Giant took no notice of the tiny voice, and went on making his ropes of sand.

The little Piskey then got into his ear and poked his red-capped head into the hollow of it, and again shouted:

'I am the little Piskey who told you he had lost his laugh, and——'

Piskey in Search of his Laugh

' Ah ! the dinky little fellow who tried to help me
to find my soul,' interrupted the great Giant, in a
voice almost as loud as the waves breaking on the
Padstow Doombar.

' Yes,' answered the Piskey, ' and a dinky Little
Bargeman brought me from Dozmare Pool to
Trebetherick that you might answer my question.'

' I know who you mean — Merlin, the little old
Master of Magic,' cried the Giant in evident astonishment, pausing in his work of making a rope of sand
to stare at the little Piskey. ' Fancy his bringing a
tiny brown fellow like you from Dozmare Pool to
Trebetherick Bay in his Magic Barge ! Pigs will fly
and sing after this !'

' He saw me helping you to dip the pool dry, and
said that one kind deed deserved another,' said the
Piskey as meek as a harvest-mouse. ' So he brought
me all the way down to St. Minver to know if you
had seen my laugh. Have you seen it, Mister Giant ?'

' No, I have not seen it,' answered the Giant.
' Nothing so cheerful as a Piskey's laugh would come
near such a mountain of misery as I am ; and if by
an evil chance it did come, it would flee far from my
dark shadow.'

' Do you know anyone else who has seen my
laugh ?' asked the little Piskey piteously.

' Not one ; unless your cousins, the Night-riders,
have,' answered the Giant, looking at the sand-ropes
he had just finished, lying at his feet. ' I must now
begin to bind my trusses of sand.'

North Cornwall Fairies

He stooped to lift them as he spoke, and as he tried to take them up they fell to pieces in his hand. As they crumbled away his face was awful to see, and he began to howl and roar, and his cries of rage rang out over the sand-hills and over Trebetherick Bay, and were heard above the noise of waves breaking on the Padstow Doombar.

Those roars of rage and anger so frightened the people living in the villages in the neighbourhood of the common that they shook in their beds, and as for the little Piskey, he was so terrified by what he had heard and seen that he tumbled over the hillock up which he had climbed to get into the Giant's ear.

When he had picked himself up, Giant Tregeagle was flying away like an evil bird towards the south.

The dawn broke soon after the Giant had gone, and as Piskeys always hide by day, he hid himself under a clump of tamarisk, and stayed there till the dark and the stars came again. When he came out he remembered what the Giant had said—that perhaps his cousins, the Night-riders, had seen his laugh. The moon being several days older than when the kind little Lantern Man had taken him to Dozmare Pool, it was now shining brightly over the common, and he knew if the Night-riders were in the neighbourhood of the sand-hills they would soon be riding over the common.

As he was gazing about with wistful eyes a young colt came galloping along with scores of little Night-

'Night-riders, Night-riders, please stop!'

THE NEW YORK
PUBLIC LIBRARY

ASTOR, LENOX AND
TILDEN FOUNDATIONS

riders astride his back, and as many more hanging on to his mane and tail.

The Night-riders, who were little people no bigger than Piskeys, and quite as mischievous, had taken the colt from a farmer's stable close to the common, and were enjoying their stolen ride as only Night-riders could.

As they and the colt drew near, the little Piskey stood out in the moonshine and shouted:

'Night-riders, Night-riders, please stop! I want to ask you something.'

But the little Night-riders were enjoying their gallop too much to listen or stop, and they flew by like the wind.

The colt was fresh, and galloped like mad, and soon went round the common and back again; and as he was galloping by, the Piskey once more shouted to the little Night-riders to stop, but they took no heed, and once more flew by like the wind.

Ever so many times the colt galloped round the sandy common, leaping over the hillocks in his mad gallop, and each time he passed, the little Piskey stood out in the moonshine and called out, but the Night-riders took not the slightest notice, nor pulled up the colt to see what he wanted.

At last, when the Piskey had given up all hope of the Night-riders stopping, the colt, who was quite worn out with galloping so hard round and round the broken common, put his foot into a rabbit-hole and came down with a crash, with his many little riders on top of him.

One little Night-rider, who happened to be astride the colt's left ear, was pitched off at the Piskey's feet.

He looked as bright as a robin in his little red riding-coat, brown leggings, and his bright green cap with a wren's feather stuck in its front.

When he had picked himself up, he thrust his tiny brown hands into his breeches pocket, stared hard at the little Piskey, and cried:

' What wisht little beggar are you ?'

' I am a poor little chap who has lost his laugh,' answered the Piskey. ' I shouted every time you galloped the colt past here to ask if you had seen it, but you never stopped.'

' Of course we did not stop galloping because a Piskey called,' said the little Night-rider. ' How came you to be such a gawk as to lose your laugh ?'

' I have no idea,' the Piskey returned. ' I only know it went away all of a sudden, and I have been searching for it ever since. Have you seen my little lost laugh ?'

' No; but Granfer Night-rider may have,' answered the little Night-rider. ' He has wonderful eyes for seeing things that are lost.'

' Is Granfer Night-rider here ?' asked the Piskey, sending his glance in the direction of the colt, which was almost smothered with Night-riders, some standing on his side as he lay, others still in the stirrups they had made in his tail and mane.

Piskey in Search of his Laugh

'He was on top of the colt's tail a minute ago,' answered the little Night-rider, following the Piskey's glance. 'There he is,' pointing to a tiny old fellow with a bushy grey beard coming towards them, carrying a tamarisk switch in his hand, with which he lashed the air as he came. He wore a red riding-coat, green breeches, red cap and feather like the other little Night-riders.

'What woebegone little rascal are you?' asked the old Greybeard, staring hard at the Piskey.

'A Piskey who has lost his laugh,' answered the little Night-rider for him, 'and he had the impertinence to want us to stop galloping to tell him if we had seen it.'

'You were very foolish to lose your laugh,' said Granfer Night-rider, standing in front of the unhappy little Piskey. 'How did you manage to lose it?'

And the poor little fellow, without lifting his eyes from the sandy ground, told him.

'You are in Queer Lane, my son,' said Granfer Night-rider, when he had told him how he had lost his laugh, 'and I would not give a grain of corn for you.'

'Wouldn't you?' wailed the poor little Piskey.

'No, I wouldn't, nor half a grain either.'

Quite a crowd of scarlet-coated little Night-riders had gathered near the Piskey by this time, and had listened to all that was said, and one little Night-rider asked if a Piskey had ever had the misfortune to lose his laugh before.

'Yes, once in the long ago,' answered the old Greybeard, fixing his eye on the little Piskey, who trembled beneath his gaze, ' and what was worse still, he never found it again. And so very unhappy was that little fellow without his laugh, and so miserable did he make everybody with his bewailings, that at last the Piskey tribe to which he belonged sent out a command that whoever found him wandering about the country was to take him in charge as a Piskey vagrant, put him into a Piskey-bag, and hang him upside down like a widdy-mouse in the first cavern they came to. He was found, put into a Piskey-bag, and hung up in a cavern. There he is still, and there he will hang till there are no more Small People!'

' Has the order yet been given for *this* little Piskey vagrant to be taken up and treated in like manner?' asked another little Night-rider.

The poor little Piskey did not wait to hear the answer, but took to his heels and ran as fast as he could to the north, and the little Night-riders who were still standing on the colt watched him till he was out of sight, and Granfer Night-rider and all the other little Night-riders yelled after him to stop, but he did not stop.

The Piskey ran and ran, and he never stopped running till he came to Castle Gardens, whence he had started.

When he got there he was as exhausted as a colt ridden all night by naughty Night-riders, and he sank down all of a heap by the side of a mole-hill, where two tiny hands were again sticking up.

'Is your ladyship under the hill?' asked the little Piskey when he could speak.

'Yes,' answered the mole. 'Who are you?'

'The little Piskey who lost his laugh.'

'What! haven't you found it yet?'

'No,' he answered sadly, 'and I am dreadfully afraid I never shall. If I don't find it soon I shall be taken up for a Piskey vagrant, put in a bag, and hung upside down like a widdy-mouse in some cavern.'

'That will be a very tragic ending to a bright little Piskey,' said the mole. 'Tell me how you know that that will be your fate if you don't find your laugh.'

And the Piskey told her. In fact, the Lady Want was so interested about what Granfer Night-rider had said that she begged him to tell her all his adventures from the time he set out to Rough Tor Marsh in search of his laugh till his return to Castle Gardens, which he was quite glad to do.

'You ought to find your laugh after all your travels and what you have gone through,' said the Lady Want when he had related everything, 'and I hope you will.'

'Does your ladyship happen to know anybody else who may have seen my laugh?' asked the little Piskey wistfully.

'Only one.'

'And who may that one be?' queried the little Piskey. 'Will your ladyship be kind enough to tell me?'

'The Good King Arthur,' the mole answered in a low voice.

'Good King Arthur!' ejaculated the Piskey. 'Why, he is dead, and a dead King is no more good than a Piskey without his laugh.'

'King Arthur is not dead,' said the mole.

'Not dead!' echoed the little Piskey in great surprise.

'No; he was seen perched only last evening on his own seat, which is still called King Arthur's Seat, and which, as I dare say you know, overhangs the sea.'

'Arthur the King not dead!' whispered the little Piskey, as if he could not get over his amazement.

'A precious good thing for you he isn't,' snapped the mole.

'But how isn't he dead?' asked the little Piskey.

'Because he was changed by magic into a bird,' answered the mole; 'he haunts the Dundagel* cliffs and the ruins of his old castle in the form of a chough. He was wounded almost unto death in his last great battle, it is true,' she added, for the small man looked as if he wanted this strange happening fully explained, 'and the marks of the battle he fought and the hurts he received are yet upon him, as the legs and beak of the great black bird plainly show—as plainly as my own

* Tintagel.

44

tiny hands that I was once a great lady. But he is still alive. If you should see a bird with a red beak and legs flying over King Arthur's Castle as day is beginning to break, you may be quite certain that he is King Arthur. If he has seen your laugh he will be sure to tell you. He is very kind and good, as all the world knows.'

'*Which is still called King Arthur's Seat.*'

'I am glad the Good King is not dead,' said the little Piskey. 'I'll try and keep awake till the dawn so that I can ask him about my laugh; but I am so tired.'

The little fellow did his best to keep awake, but he was too worn out with his run from St. Minver sand-hills to Tintagel Castle to sit and watch for the

coming of the red-legged bird ; and long before the
sun wheeled up behind the Tors and shone upon the
sea he was sound asleep under a great mallow growing by one of the grey old walls. When he awoke
a day and a night had come and gone, and the birth
of a new day was at hand.

When he crawled out from under the mallow, the
first thing he saw on the Island facing him was the
dark form of a great black chough. He was perched
on the wall above the old arched doorway, gazing
gravely in front of him.

The Piskey lost not a moment in getting across to
the Island, which he did by the Piskey passage known
only to the Piskeys ; and when he had caught the
bird's attention he said :

'I am a poor little Piskey who has lost his laugh,
and I am come to ask the Good King Arthur if he
has seen it.'

But the bird was too high up for him to make
himself heard, and he had to wait patiently till it
flew down. After waiting a short time it did, and
perched on a stick stuck in the ground.

The Piskey ran over, and, clasping his hands, he
repeated what he had just said.

'How came you to know I was King Arthur ?'
asked the chough, ignoring the little fellow's question.

'The mole who says she is the Lady Want told
me,' he answered.

'Ah, I know her—the grand lady who considered

the ground on which she walked was not good enough for her dainty feet, and has now, as a punishment, to walk under the ground—a lesson to all children of pride.'

'But please, Good King Arthur, answer my question about my laugh,' pleaded the little Piskey, in an agony of impatience. 'If I don't find it soon something dreadful will happen to me.'

'Have patience,' said the chough kindly. 'Nothing is ever won by impatience. I have seen something very funny lately running about over the grass. It is like nothing I have ever seen before except in a Piskey's face when he laughs. It is like a laugh gone mad, and it is enough to kill a man with laughing only to watch its antics. It made me laugh till I ached when I first noticed it. It does not make a sound, but its grimaces are worth flying a hundred miles only to see.'

'It must have been my laugh you saw,' cried the Piskey—'my dear little lost laugh that I have travelled so far to find. Where is it now, Good King Arthur?'

'It was here not long since,' answered the bird, who did not deny that he was Arthur the King. 'Why, there it is quite close to you,' pointing with his long-pointed beak to the most comical-looking thing you ever saw, on the grass a foot from where the Piskey was standing. 'It was a laugh gone mad,' as the chough said.

The Piskey looked behind him, and when he saw

47

the little bit of laughing, grinning absurdity on the grass, he jumped for joy and shrieked: 'It is my own little laugh that I lost!'

Holding out both his arms, he cried, 'Oh, dear little laugh, come back to me! Oh, dear little laugh, come back to me!' And the droll little thing, which was a grin with a laugh and a laugh with a grin, came over to the Piskey, and began to climb up his legs, grinning and doubling itself up with laughter as it climbed, till it reached his chin, when it narrowed itself into a tiny grin and vanished into the Piskey.

The next moment the Piskey was shouting at the top of his voice, 'I have got my laugh! I have got my laugh!' and he ran off laughing and dancing to the edge of the cliff and disappeared into the Piskey-hole, and in a few minutes more he was on Castle Gardens in the great Piskey-ring, laughing and dancing and dancing and laughing.

His laugh was so loud and so free that his brother Piskeys heard him from afar, and came running over the cliffs from Bossiney to see what ever had happened.

Little Fiddler Piskey was the first to reach the Gardens, and the first glance at the little whirling figure told him that his little brother had found his laugh; and putting his fiddle in position, he began fiddling away as hard as he could.

As he fiddled, the other Piskeys, including Granfer Piskey, reached the ring, and the next minute they were all dancing and laughing as they had never laughed and danced before; but the one who laughed the heartiest was the little Piskey who had lost and found his laugh.

They danced for a good hour, the little fiddler in their midst fiddling his fiddle, all the while keeping time with his head and foot, heedless that the daylight was driving the darkness away to the country to which it belongs; and King Arthur the Bird flew up on the wall and watched, and the mole who called herself the Lady Want let her dainty hands be seen on the mole-hill, till the fiddling, dancing, and laughing were finished, and the Piskeys went off to the Piskey-beds to sleep.

The Legend of the Padstow Doombar

The Legend of the Padstow Doombar

Lifeboat going over the bar of doom.

IN a far-away time Tristram Bird of Padstow bought a gun at a little shop in the quaint old market which in those days opened to the quay, the winding river, and the St. Minver sandhills. When he had bought his gun he began forthwith to shoot birds and other poor little creatures.

After a while he grew more ambitious, and told the fair young maids of Padstow that he wanted to shoot a seal or something more worthy of his gun; and so one bright morning he made his way down to Hawker's Cove, near the mouth of the harbour.

North Cornwall Fairies

When Tristram got there he looked about him to see what he could shoot, and the first thing he saw was a young maid sitting all alone on a rock, combing her hair with a sea-green comb.

He was so overcome at such an unexpected sight that he quite forgot what had brought him to the cove, and could do nothing but stare.

The rock on which the maiden sat was covered with seaweed, and surrounded by a big pool, called in that distant time the Mermaid's Glass.

She was apparently unconscious that a good-looking young man was gazing at her with his bold dark eyes, and as she combed her long and beautiful hair she leaned over the pool and looked at herself in the Mermaid's Glass, and the face reflected in it was startling in its beauty and charm.

Tristram Bird was very tall—six feet three in his stockings—and being such a tall young man, he could see over the maiden's head into the pool, and the face in its setting of golden hair reflected in its clear depths entirely bewitched him, and so did her graceful form, which was partly veiled in a golden raiment of her own beautiful hair.

As he stood gazing at the bewitching face looking up from the Mermaid's Glass, its owner suddenly glanced over her shoulder, and saw Tristram staring at her.

'Good-morning to you, fair maid,' he said, still keeping his bold dark eyes fixed upon her, telling

Tristram Bird could see over the maiden's head into the pool.

THE NEW YORK
PUBLIC LIBRARY

ASTOR, LENOX AND
TILDEN FOUNDATIONS.
C   L.

himself as he gazed that her face was even more
bewitching than was its reflection.

'Good-morning, sir,' said she.

'Doing your toilet out in the open,' he said.

'Yes,' quoth she, wondering who the handsome
youth could be and how he came to be there.

'Your hair is worth combing,' he said.

'Is it?' said she.

'It is, my dear,' he said. ''Tis the colour of oats
waiting for the sickle.'

'Is it?' quoth she.

'Yes; and no prettier face ever looked into the
Mermaid's Glass.'

'How do you know?' asked she.

'My heart told me so,' he said, coming a step or
two nearer the pool, 'and so did my eyes when I
saw its reflection looking up from the water. It
bewitched me, sweet.'

'Did it?' laughed she, with a tilt of her round
young chin.

'Yes,' he said, with an answering laugh, drawing
another step nearer the pool.

'It does not take a man of your breed long to fall
in love,' said the beautiful maid, with a toss of her
golden head and a curl of her sweet red lips.

'Who told you that?' asked the love-sick young
man, going red as a poppy.

'Faces carry tales as well as little birds,' quoth
she.

'If my face is a tale-bearer, it will tell you that I

love you more than heart can say and tongue can tell,' he said, drawing yet nearer the pool.

'Will it?' said she, combing her golden hair with her sea-green comb.

'Indeed it will, and must,' he said; 'for I love you with all my soul, and I want you to give me a lock of your golden hair to wear over my heart.'

'I do not give locks of my hair to landlubbers!' cried she, with another toss of her proud young head and a scornful curl of her bright red lips.

'A landlubber forsooth!' he said, with an angry flash in his bold black eyes. 'Who are you to speak so scornfully of a man of the land? One would think you were a maid of the sea.'

'I am,' quoth she, twining the tress of her hair she had combed round her shell-pink arm.

'No seamaid is half as beautiful as you,' said Tristram Bird, incredulous of what the maid said. 'But, maid of the sea or maid of the land, I love you, sweet, and I want to have you to wife.'

'Want must be your master, sir,' said she, with an angry flash in her sea-blue eyes.

'Love is my master, sweet maid,' he said. 'You are my love, and you have mastered me.'

'Have I?' said she, with a little toss of her golden head.

'Yes,' he said; 'and now that I have told you you are my love, and I want you to marry me, you will give me a lock of your golden hair, won't you, sweet?'

The Legend of Padstow Doombar

' I cannot,' said she.

'Give me one little golden wire of your hair, if you won't give me a lock,' he pleaded, coming close to the edge of the pool. ' I will make a golden ring of it,' he said, ' and wear it in the eye of the world.'

' Will you ?' said she.

' I will, my dear,' he said.

' But I will not give you a hair of my head even to make a ring with,' said she.

' Then give me one for a leading-string,' he said. ' If you will, my charmer, you shall take the end of it and lead me whithersoever you will.'

' Even to the whipping-post ?' said she.

' Even to the whipping-post,' he said. ' So you will be my fair bride, won't 'ee, sweet ? If you will consent to love me, I'll make you as happy as the day is long.'

' Will you ?' cried she, with a warning look in her sea-blue eyes and a strange little laugh.

' Yes,' he said, thinking her answer meant consent. 'And I've got a dear little house at Higher St. Saviour's, overlooking the river and Padstow Town low in the valley.'

' Have you ?' said she.

' I have,' he said. ' And the little house is full of handsome things—a chestful of linen which my own mother wove for me on her loom against the time I should be wed to a pretty maid like you, an oaken dresser with every shelf full of cloam,* and a cosy

* China.

settle where we can sit hand in hand talking of our
love. You will marry me soon, won't you, sweet ?
The little house, and all that's in it, is waiting for
my charmer.'

' Is it ?' cried the beautiful maid, taking up another
tress of her golden hair, and slowly combing its
silken length with her sea-green comb. ' But let
me tell you once and for ever, I would not marry
you if you were decked in diamonds and your house
a golden house, and everything in it made of jewels
and set in gold.'

' Wouldn't you ?' cried Tristram Bird, in great
amazement.

' I wouldn't,' said she.

' You are a strange young maid to refuse an up-
standing young man like me,' he said, 'who has a
house of his own, to say nothing of what is inside it.
Why, dozens of fair young maidens up to Padstow
would have me to-morrow if I was only to ax them.'

' Then ax *them*,' cried the beautiful maid, turning
her proud young head, and looking out towards
Pentire, gorgeous in its spring colouring.

' But I can't ask any of them to marry me when I
love *you*,' cried the infatuated youth. ' You have
bewitched me, sweet, and no other man shall have
you. If I can't have you living, I'll have you dead.
I came down to Hawker's Cove to shoot something
to startle the natives of Padstow Town, and they
will be startled, shure 'nough, if I shoot a beautiful
little vixen like you and take home to them.'

The Legend of Padstow Doombar

'Shoot me if you will, but marry you I will not,' said the beautiful maiden, with a scornful laugh. 'But I give you fair warning that if you shoot me, as you say you will, you will rue the day you did your wicked deed. I will curse you and this beautiful haven, which has ever been a refuge for ships from the time that ships sailed upon the seas;' and her sea-blue eyes looked up and down the estuary from the headlands that guarded its mouth to the farthest point of the blue, winding river.

'I will shoot you in spite of the curse if you won't consent to be mine,' cried the bewitched young man.

'I will never consent,' said she.

'Then I will shoot you now,' he said, and Tristram Bird lifted his gun and fired, and the ball entered the poor young maiden's soft pink side.

She put her hand to her side to cover the gaping wound the shot had made, and as she did so she pulled herself out of the water, and where the feet should have been was the glittering tail of a fish!

'I have shot a poor young Mermaid,' Tristram cried, 'and woe is me!' and he shivered like one when somebody is passing over his grave.

'Yes, you have shot a poor Mermaid,' said the maid of the sea, 'and I am dying, and with my dying breath I curse this safe harbour, which was large enough to hold all the fighting ships of the Spanish Armada and your own, and it shall be cursed with a bar of sand which shall be a bar of doom to many a stately ship and many a noble life, and it shall

stretch from the Mermaid's Glass to Trebetherick
Bay on the opposite shore, and prevent this haven
of deep water from ever again becoming a floating
harbour save at full tide. The Mermaid's wraith
will haunt the bar of doom her dying curse shall
bring until your wicked deed has been fully avenged :'
and looking round the great bay of shining waters,

Trebetherick Bay.

laughing and rippling in the eye of the sun, she
raised her arms and cursed the harbour of Padstow
with a bitter curse, and Tristram shuddered as he
listened, and as she cursed she uttered a wailing cry
and fell back dead into the pool, and the water where
she sank was dyed with her blood.

'I have committed a wicked deed,' said Tristram
Bird, gazing into the blood-stained pool, 'and verily

The Legend of Padstow Doombar

I shall be punished for my sin;' and he turned away with the fear of coming doom in his heart.

As he went up the cove and along the top of the cliffs the distressful, wailing cry of the Mermaid seemed to follow him, and the sky gloomed all around as he went, and the sea moaned a dreadful moan as it came up the bay.

When he reached Tregirls, overlooking the Cove, he stood by the gate for a minute and gazed out over the beautiful harbour. The sea, which only half an hour ago was as blue as the eyes of the seamaid he had shot, and full of smiles and laughter, was now black as ash-buds, save where a golden streak lay across the water from Hawker's Cove to Trebetherick Bay.

'The Mermaid's curse is already working,' moaned Tristram Bird, and he fled through the lane leading to Padstow as if a death-hound was after him.

When he reached Place House he met a little crowd of Padstow maids going out flower-gathering.

'Whither away so fast, Tristram Bird?' asked a little maid. 'You aren't driving a teem of snails this time, 'tis plain to see. Where hast thou been?'

'Need you ask?' said a pert young girl. 'He has been away shooting something to startle the maids of Padstow with! What strange new creature did you shoot, Tristram Bird?'

'A wonderful creature with eyes like blue fire,' returned the unhappy youth, looking away over

North Cornwall Fairies

St. Minver dunes towards the Tors—'a sweet, soft creature with beautiful hair, every wire of which was a sunbeam of gold, and her face was the loveliest I ever beheld. It clean bewitched me.'

'A beautiful maid like that, and yet you shot her?' cried all the young maids of Padstow Town.

'Yes, I shot her, to my undoing and the undoing of our fair haven,' groaned Tristram Bird; and he told them all about it—where he had seen the beautiful Mermaid, of his bewitchment from the moment he saw her face of haunting charm looking up at him from the Mermaid's Glass, and of the curse she uttered ere she fell back dead into the pool.

All the smiles went out of the bright faces of the Padstow maids, as he told his tale.

'What a pity, Tristram Bird, you should have been so foolish as to shoot a Mermaid!' they said; and they did not go and pick flowers as they had intended, but went back to their homes instead, and Tristram Bird went on to Higher St. Saviour's, where he lived in a little house overlooking Padstow Town nestling like a bird in its nest.

A fearful gale blew on the night of the day Tristram Bird shot the Mermaid, and all the next day, too, and the next night; and through the awful howling of the gale was heard the bellowing of the wind-tormented sea.

Such a terrible storm had never been known at Padstow Town within the memory of man, so the

64

The Legend of Padstow Doombar

old Granfer men said, and never a gale lasted so long.

When the wind went down the natives of Padstow ventured out to see what the gale had wrought, and sad was the havoc it had made; and some went out to Chapel Stile, where a small chapel stood overlooking the haven, and what should meet their horrified gaze but a terrible bar of sand which the

Chapel Stile.

Mermaid's curse had brought there; and it stretched from Hawker's Cove to the opposite shore, and what was worse, the great sand-bar was covered with wrecks of ships and bodies of drowned men.

'It is the bar of doom brought there by the fearful curse of the maid of the sea whom I shot with my brand-new gun,' cried Tristram Bird, who was one of the first to reach the stile when the wind had gone down; and he told them all, as he had told the Padstow maids, of what the Mermaid had said before and after he had shot her. 'And because of the wicked deed I did,' he said, 'I have brought a curse on my native town, and Padstow will never be blessed with a safe and beautiful harbour till the poor Mermaid's death be avenged.'

There was a dreadful silence after Tristram Bird had spoken, and the men and women of Padstow Town gazed at each other, troubled and sad, knowing that what the youth, who had been bewitched by the Mermaid's face, had said was true, for there below them was the great bar of sand dividing the outer harbour from the inner, and on it lay the masts and spars of broken ships and the lifeless bodies of the drowned. The wind was quiet, but the sea was still breaking and roaring on the back of the Doombar, and as the waves thundered and broke, a wailing cry sounded forth. like the wail that Tristram heard when the Mermaid disappeared under the water; it sounded like the distressful cry of a woman bewailing her dead, and all who heard shivered and shook, and both old and young looked down on the Doombar with dread in their eyes, but they saw nothing but the dead bodies of the sailors and their broken ships.

'It is the Mermaid's wraith,' cried an old Granfer man, leaning against the grey walls of the ancient chapel, 'and she is wailing the wail of the drowned; and, mark my words, everyone,' letting his

'*It is the Mermaid's wraith,' cried an old Granfer man.*

THE NEW YORK
PUBLIC LIBRARY

ASTOR, LENOX AND
TILDEN FOUNDATIONS.

The Legend of Padstow Doombar

eyes wander from one face to another, 'each time a
ship is caught on this dreadful bar and lives are lost
—as lost they will be—the Mermaid's wraith will
bewail the drowned.'

    *   *   *   *   *

And it came to pass as the old man said, and
whenever vessels are wrecked on that fateful bar of
sand lying across the mouth of Padstow Harbour
and men are drowned, it is told that the Mermaid's
distressful cry is still heard bewailing the poor dead
sailors.

The Little Cake-bird

The Little Cake-bird

Tregoss Moor.

ON the Tregoss Moors, where in the long-ago
King Arthur and his Noble Knights went
a-hunting, was a quaint old thatched cottage
built of moorstone, and in it lived an old woman
called Tamsin Tredinnick and her little grand-
daughter Phillida; it stood between Castle-an-Dinas
—a great camp-crowned hill—and the far-famed
Roche Rocks.

It possessed only one room, which, fortunately,

was fairly large, for it had to contain most of old Tamsin's possessions, including a low wooden bedstead, an old oak dresser, a hutch for the grail —a coarse flour of which she made bread for herself and little Phillida—and her spinning-wheel.

At the side of the cottage was a small linhey, or outhouse, the door of which the old woman always kept open in inclement weather that the wild creatures of the moors might take shelter from the cold and from the storms that swept over the great exposed moorland spaces.

Tamsin was very poor, and could only earn enough to pay the rent of her cottage and to keep herself and little grandchild, who was an orphan, in grail-bread and coarse clothes. This she did by spinning wool, which she sold to a wool-merchant at St. Columb, a small market-town some miles away. She was advanced in years, and getting more unfit to spin every year, she told herself; and the less wool she spun the less money she had to spend on food and clothes for herself and Phillida. But, poor as she was, she was honest and good, and so was her little orphaned grandchild. They seldom complained, and when things were at their worst, and there was no grail left to make bread, or money to buy any, they told each other they had what bettermost people had not—wide moors to look out upon, and pure moorland air, fragrant with moor-flowers, to breathe into their lungs, little birds to sing to them most of the year, and dear little Piskeys

The Little Cake-bird

to laugh outside their window in the dusk when they were very wisht.*

Tamsin was a child of Nature, and she loved the big, lonely moors, gorgeous with broom and gorse in the spring-time and fading bracken in the autumn months, with all her simple heart, and so did little

On the way to Tamsin's Cottage.

Phillida. They loved all the moor-flowers—even the duller blossoms of the mint and nettle tribes—that made those great, lonely spaces so wonderful and so full of charm. There was not a flower that broke into beautiful life on the moors but had a place in

* Sad.

their hearts. They were their near and dear relations, they said, and as for the birds and other creatures that lived on the moorland, they were to them, as to St. Francis, their brothers and sisters, and even the Piskeys—the Cornish fairies—had a warm place in their affections.

Not a great way from Tamsin's cottage was a large Piskey Circle where the Tregoss Piskeys danced when the nights were fine and the moon was up, and often when they danced the old grandmother and her little grandmaid would come out on the step of their door and watch them.

They could see the Piskey Circle quite distinctly from the doorstep, and the Piskey-lights which the Piskeys held in their hands when they danced. But they never saw the Piskeys, for the Dinky Men, as Phillida called them, were very shy, and did not often let themselves be seen by human eyes. The old woman and the child never ventured near their Circle when the Small People were having their high flings, partly from a feeling of delicacy, and partly for fear of driving them away. The Dinky Men were as touchy as nesting-birds, Tamsin declared, and said that if either she or Phillida spied upon them when they were having their frolics they would, perhaps, forsake Tregoss Moor, which would have been a great misfortune. It was lucky, she said, to have the Small People living near a house. So she and her grandchild were content to watch them dancing from a respectable distance.

The Little Cake-bird

The place where the Piskeys made their Circle
was very smooth and soft with grass, and the Circle
lay upon the close, thick turf like a red-gold ring.
Behind the Circle was a small granite boulder, and
above the boulder a big furze-bush, which burnt like
a fire when the furze was in bloom, and there little
yellow-hammers sang their little songs year in and
year out.

The Tregoss Moor Piskeys were quite nice for
Piskeys, and took a great interest in Phillida and
her old grandmother. They never tried to Piskey-
lead them into the bogs and stream-works, of which
there were many on the moors, nor set up Piskey-
lights to slock * them into the Piskey Circle, which,
we must confess, they did to their betters when they
had the chance. They were ever so sorry when
they knew the grail-hutch was getting empty, which
somehow they always did, and that Grannie Tredinnick, as they called her, because Phillida did, had
no money to buy grail to fill it; and they hastened to
the cottage and peeped through the window and keyhole to see if they were looking wisht, and if they
were they would begin to laugh in order to cheer
them up and make them forget how hungry and sad
they were.

A Piskey's laugh is a gay little laugh, and as un-
fettered as the song of a lark, and anybody hearing
it is bound to feel happy and gay, no matter how
wisht he happens to be before. Perhaps that is the

* Coax.

77

reason the old saying 'laughing like a Piskey' is so often quoted in the Cornish land.

Old Tamsin and little Phillida always felt better when the Dinky Men came and laughed outside their door. Their laugh acted like a charm on the old woman, and often after the Piskeys came and laughed she laughed too, because she could not help it, and she would forget her aches and her pains, and would go to the spinning-wheel and try to spin. She generally found she could, and soon spun enough wool to buy grail to fill the grail-hutch.

Tamsin suffered from rheumatism, and when the weather was very wet and raw on the moors her hands and feet were crippled with pain; she could not spin at all, and not even the Piskeys' gay little laughs could charm the pain out of them.

One autumn and the beginning of the following winter were unusually wet, and the old woman's rheumatism was very bad, and, what was worse still, the Dinky Men went away from the moors. Where they had gone she did not know, and fervently hoped that she and Phillida had not offended them in any way.

The hum of the spinning-wheel was silent as the grave, the grail-hutch was empty, and they had had to feed on berries like the birds. When things were at their worst the clouds left off raining, the weather brightened, the sun shone out, and the little brown Piskeys came back to the moors. Finding out how matters were in the little moorland cottage, they

The Little Cake-bird

came outside the door and laughed their gay little laugh once more. They laughed so much and so funnily that Grannie Tredinnick, weak as she was, couldn't help laughing to save her life ; and when they saw her rise up from her chair and go over to the spinning-wheel and make the wheel whirl, they were delighted and laughed again.

The weather not only changed for the better, but warm soft days came, and the yellow-hammers and the black and white stone-chats must have thought summer had come again, and they sang their bright little songs, and the larks went up singing into the blue of the winter sky. Tamsin felt better than she had been for months, and became so well and cheerful, what with the brighter weather, the music of the birds, and the free laughter of the Dinky Men, that she was able to spin from morning shine till evening dark, and very soon she had spun all the wool she had. She sent it in a farmer's cart to St. Columb, and the farmer's man who took it for her brought back a great big bag of flour and some more wool to spin. But when that was all paid for, and the rent money put aside, all her earnings were gone, which made the good old woman very sad, for she wanted to make a little Christmas cake for Phillida.

Christmas was on its way, and Phillida, like most children, looked forward to it ; why, she could hardly have told, except that it was the Great Festival of the Nativity, and that Grannie always told her of the nice Christmasses she had had when she was a croom * of a cheeld, and that her mother always made her a Christmas cake, with a little bird on top, to remind her of the Great White Birds which sang when the Babe was born.

When Christmas drew near Phillida could think and talk of nothing else but the beautiful Christmasses Grannie had had when she was a little maid, and of the Christmas cake with the little bird on top her mother had made for her. A few days before Christmas, as she and her grandmother were sitting down to their dinner of grail-bread, she said :

'Christmas Eve will soon be here now, Grannie. Do you think you can make me a little Christmas cake with a little cake-bird on top like those you had ? Ever such a dinky cake and ever such a dinky bird will do, Grannie,' she added, as the old woman shook her head, 'just to see what a Christmas cake tastes like and the little cake-bird looks like.'

' I would gladly make 'ee a cake and a little bird,' said Tamsin, 'if only I was rich ; but I am afraid I can't afford to make 'ee even a dinky one. You can't buy sugar and spice and other things to make a cake without money, and I ent a got no money, not even a farthing.'

'Haven't you?' cried little Phillida, her sweet child eyes full of tears. ' I am so disappointed, Grannie ; I did so hope you could afford just a dinky cake.'

' I had hoped so, too, cheeld,' said the kind old woman. ' Never mind, I'll ask the Piskeys to come

* Tiny child.

The Little Cake-bird

in and order you a little dream-cake an' a little dream-bird.'

'What is a little dream-cake, Grannie, and a little dream-bird?' asked the child.

'The Piskeys used to come in through the keyhole to pass over the bridges of children's noses, when I was a little maid like you, to order their dreams. It would be ever so nice if they passed over the bridge of your nose and ordered you a little dream-cake and a little dream-bird.'

'But you can't eat cakes in your dreams,' said little Phillida, 'and you can't hold little dream-birds in your hands.'

'Can't you?' cried Grannie. 'That's all you know about it. I will ask the Dinky Men to come through our keyhole to order your dreams the very next time they are outside our cottage.'

'They are outside now,' said Phillida. 'I hear them laughing. Listen, Grannie!' And the old woman listened, and she knew that the child was right, and that the Piskeys were outside their window, for she too heard their laughter.

'The Dinky Men be there right enough,' said Tamsin, 'an' they are tickled about something, by the way they are laughing.'

'P'raps they heard what you said about asking them to come in and order me a little dream-cake and a little dream-bird,' suggested the little maid.

'I shouldn't wonder,' laughed Grannie; 'an' I'm sure they'll be willing. I'll ask them now;' and getting up from her wooden arm-chair, she went to the door and called softly : ' Little Piskeys, are you there ?'

But the Piskeys made no response to the old woman's question save by a gay little laugh.

' If you be there, an' can hear me,' said Tamsin, ' I want 'ee to be so good as to come through my key-hole on the evening of Christmas Eve an' pass over the bridge of Phillida's nose, an' order her a little dream-cake with a little dream-bird on top. I shall be so obliged to 'ee if you will, for I am too poor to make the cheeld a real cake an' a little cake-bird.'

When the old woman had said all this, such a burst of laughter broke on the winter air outside the cottage that Phillida rushed to the door and looked out.

She could not see the Dinky Men, but their laughter was more than enough to tell her that they were there, and Grannie said she was sure they had heard what she asked, and would do it gladly.

As they stood on their doorstep they heard the sound of tiny tripping feet going away from the cottage in the direction of the Piskey Circle ; and as they followed the sound they noticed how bright the Circle was on the soft green turf.

It was a perfect day—one of those very rare days we are privileged to have once or twice in December month—and the moors were full of charm. The many pools on it were full of light, the boulder near the Piskey Circle was diamond bright in the sun-

'*I hear them laughing. Listen, Grannie!*'

THE NEW YORK
PUBLIC LIBRARY

ASTOR, LENOX AND
TILDEN FOUNDATIONS.

The Little Cake-bird

shine, and above it the furze was already breaking
into golden blossom. The purple had 'pulsed' out
of the heath and the pink from the ling, but each
little sprig was a marvel of brown, and showed up
the silver lichen that splashed the brown. The

The Roche Rocks.

bracken was brilliant in warm tones of orange and
gold, the brambles were every shade of crimson and
red, and the haze on the moors was like the bloom
of the hurts,* which still supplied food for the birds

* Whortleberries.

85

on the hills. In the direction of Roche, where the
great Roche Rocks stand in lonely solitude, six
hundred and eighty feet above the level of the sea,
with the ruins of the little chapel dedicated to holy
St. Michael on their summit, a lark went up singing
into the blue, for larks, as most observers of nature
know, are seldom out of song. The yellow-hammers
were as bright as the brightly-coloured bracken, and
sang their cheerful little lays from bramble and bush,
and the streams rippled over the moors.

The old grandmother and her little grandmaid
stood on the doorstep taking in the quiet beauty of
the moors. They even went out on to the moor,
and turned their gaze towards the Roche Rocks to
see if they could see the little sky-bird. After
listening ten minutes or longer to the lark and other
birds, and to the Piskeys laughing, they returned to
the cottage.

Fine weather seldom lasts long in winter-time,
and when Christmas Eve came it was bitterly cold.
A bitter wind blew over the moors from the north,
which brought snow in its wake, and Phillida said
the Old Woman was up in the sky picking her goose
and throwing down the feathers as fast as she could
throw them.

The child, who was healthy and strong, did not
mind the cold, and she liked watching the feathers
of the great Sky Goose whirling down on the hills
and moors ; but she was somewhat afraid the Dinky
Men would not come over the snow to order her

The Little Cake-bird

dreams. But her grandmother told her that she was certain the Small People no more minded the cold than she did, and would be sure to come in through the keyhole when they were in bed and asleep.

If Phillida did not mind the severe weather, Tamsin did. She could hardly keep herself warm in spite of a great fire that blazed on the hearthstone. Whatever else she and the child lacked, they always had a good fire to sit by, for the moors supplied them with furze and other firewood.

As it grew towards evening the old grandmother told her little grandchild about Christmas, as was her wont whenever Christmas Eve came round, and why they were told to keep it as a hallowed time. She also told her of the Christmas cakes taken hot out of the oven on Christmas Eve, and Christmas birds on top of them, which had made her Christmas so bright in those far-away years when she was young like Phillida.

Grannie's tales of the long ago were of absorbing interest to the child, who almost forgot that the Dinky Men were coming to order her dreams that night.

When the day had gone, and night had come, Tamsin banked up the fire on the hearthstone, and then she and Phillida went to bed. The old woman knew that the Piskeys would not come in through the keyhole until they were in bed and asleep.

The child and the old grandmother slept in the same bed, the latter at the head and Phillida at the foot. The head of the bed was against the wall by the side of the hearthplace, and Tamsin as she lay was in deep shadow, and only her white nightcap could be seen; but Phillida's charming little face was towards the hearth, and the fireshine fell full upon it.

The child had a fair, smooth skin and clear-cut features, and her nose had a beautiful bridge! Her hair was thick and wavy, and of a deep red gold— only a little redder than the Piskey Circle — and her eyes, when they were open, were the soft sweet blue of the Cornish Tors when the skies were grey.

The red peat and furze fire, like a Master of Magic, made the interior of the poor little moorland cottage look quite beautiful. The rough walls that went up to the brown of the thatch, where they caught the fireshine, glowed like the Small People's lanterns; the old dresser, which stood by the wall facing the hearth, looked as if it were painted in fairy colours, and the china on it glittered like the boulder near the Piskey Circle; and even the grail. hutch, a unique piece of furniture often seen in Cornish cottages, was turned into a thing of beauty. It was painted orange colour, and its little knobs were black, to which the shine of the fire gave depths and tones and undertones.

By the side of the bed where Phillida slept was a fiddle-back chair, and on its seat lay her little blue weekaday frock, that added to the quaint and

The Little Cake-bird

beautiful picture. Only a small part of the cottage was in shadow, and this intensified the brightness of the room where the firelight held sway.

The cottage was looking its brightest, and was as warm as a zam* oven, when a gay little laugh came through the keyhole, and a merry little face peeped into the room. In another minute a Dinky Man came out of the keyhole and sat on the wooden latch of the door and gazed curiously about him.

He was ever so dinky, but as cheerful-looking as a robin, in his bright red cloak and his quaint steeple hat; the face under the hat was almost as brown as an apple-pip, and only a shade or two lighter than his whiskers and beard, and his queer little eyes were full of laughter and fun.

' Are the little maid and her grannie asleep ?' called a voice through the keyhole as the Dinky Man sat on the latch surveying the room.

' I think so,' he answered. ' They are still as mice when Madam Puss is close to their hole. You are safe to come in.'

' Then in we'll come,' cried the little voice; and in the twinkling of an eye a tiny little fellow dressed in green came through the keyhole and pushed off the Dinky Man sitting on the latch, who fell on his head on old Tamsin's lime-ash floor.

Scores of little whiskered Piskeys—some in steeple hats and red flowing cloaks, some in green coats and red caps—came through the keyhole, and when they

* An oven when half heated.

had swung themselves down by the durn* of the door, they looked towards the bed.

'I'll get up on the bed and see if the little maid is really asleep,' said one of the Piskeys; and he climbed up to the top of the fiddle-back chair close to the bed and looked down on the child.

'Is she asleep?' asked the other little Piskeys eagerly.

'As sound asleep as a seven-sleeper,'† answered the Dinky Man, 'and so is Grannie Tredinnick,' sending his glance to the head of the bed. 'Get up on to the bed as soon as you like, to order the little maid's dreams—the sooner the better. We are powerless to do harm after twelve o'clock, being the night of the Birth.'

'But we have come to do good, not to do harm,' cried the Piskeys one and all, 'and we will begin at once.'

They scrambled up the legs and back of the old fiddle-back chair, and were on the bed in a quick-stick, and took their places near the sleeping child. Some sat all in a row on the edge of the patchwork quilt; some sat, or stood, on the pillow behind the child's bright little head; others were low down on the pillow; and one winking, blinking little Piskey perched himself on her arm and sat cross-legged like a tailor.

'I will be the first to order the little maid's dream,' said one of the Piskeys sitting on the edge of the

* Frame.　　　† The speckled, or ermine, moth.

The Little Cake-bird

quilt, and scrambling up, he stepped on to Phillida's
nose as light as the feathers which the old Sky Woman

*He stepped on to Phillida's nose as light as the feathers of
the old Sky Woman.*

had flung down on the moors, and as he walked over
the bridge he said :

'Dream, little maid—dream that you are wide

awake, and that you and Grannie Tredinnick are
sitting at a table covered with a cloth as white as
Piskey-wool,* and that in the middle of the table is
a lovely cake made

> ' " Of the finest of flour
> And fairy cow's cream—
> As sweet as your dream—
> And Small People's spice,
> And everything nice,
> Kneaded and mixed,
> And done in a trix
> In a little dream-bower,"

and on the top of the cake is a dinky bird with
wings spread out all ready to fly.'

Phillida dreamt as she was ordered, and in her
dream she saw the cake, and that it was a beautiful
cake, and the little cake-bird was a sweet little bird!

'What a handsome cake!' she cried out aloud in
her sleep; 'and the little cake-bird is a dear little
bird, and it looks as if it can fly and sing;' and she
laughed so heartily that the Piskeys laughed too,
and one of the Dinky Men turned head over heels
on the patchwork quilt out of sheer delight that the
child was so pleased with her beautiful dream-cake
and the little dream-bird.

'Dream that Grannie Tredinnick is as pleased
with the cake and the cake-bird as you are,' said
another little Piskey, stepping on to the bridge of
Phillida's nose, 'and that she thinks it is even

* Cotton-grass.

The Little Cake-bird

better than the cakes which were made for her when she was a croom of a cheeld, and the little cake-bird is more like a real bird than those that were on top of her Christmas cakes.'

The child dreamt as the Piskey ordered, and much beside that the Dinky Man never thought of ordering. In her dream she not only heard her grandmother say what a beautiful cake it was, and that the little cake-bird looked like a real bird, but that she said : 'We must cut and eat the cake, but spare the little cake-bird.' In her sleep she saw the old woman, dressed in her Sunday gown and cap, lean over the small oak table and cut her such a big slice of the cake that she cried out in amazed delight :

'What a great big piece you have given me, Grannie!' and her laugh was as happy and gay as a Piskey's laugh. 'But I must not eat all this myself; I must crumble some of it for the little moor-birds, and put a piece out on the doorstep for the Dinky Men. It isn't a dream-cake, Grannie, but a Christmas cake, and it has a little Christmas bird on top !'

The Piskeys looked at one another with a peculiar expression in their round little eyes when the child spoke of putting a bit of her Christmas cake on the step of the door for *them*, and one said, ' Dear little maid !' and another said ' Pretty child !' and one little fellow, with a beard reaching to his feet, cried, ' How kind of her to want us poor little Piskeys to have part in the Christmas joy !' One little Dinky

North Cornwall Fairies

Man whispered : ' Perhaps it is not true what the old whiddle* says, after all—that we are not good enough for heaven nor bad enough for hell. The child does not think so, evidently, or she would not be so anxious for us to share her little Christmas cake.'

The Piskey who sat cross-legged on Phillida's arm uncrossed his lean little legs, rose up and stepped on to her nose, and as he walked over its bridge he said ever so tenderly :

' Dream, sweet little Phillida—dream that you shared your cake with the dicky-birds, and put a piece of it on the doorstep for the Dinky Men, which they will treasure as long as there are any Dinky Men.'

The child dreamt as she was ordered, and when she had put a bit of the cake on the doorstep for the Piskeys, she saw in her dream a crowd of Dinky Men in quaint little green coats, and caps as red as bryony berries, and tiny fellows in red cloaks and green hats, come and take up the cake with solemn faces and bent heads, and carry it away over the moors towards the Piskey Circle. When they had gone, she stood on the doorstep looking out over the moors, white with the feathers the old Sky Woman had thrown down ; then she lifted her sweet little face to the sky, and saw that it was free from clouds and full of stars, which, she thought, were chiming the wonderful news of the Nativity.

* Tale.

The Little Cake-bird

She was so happy listening to the music of the Christmas stars that she forgot she had not tasted her cake till a little Piskey sprang on to her nose to turn her dream.

'Dream that you are come over to the table and eating your cake,' he said, slowly passing over the bridge of her nose.

'How can I dream that when I am out here on the doorstep listening to the ringing of the star-bells?' murmured the child in her sleep. 'I wonder if the Dinky Men like listening to the star-bells' music? They are ringing up there in the dark because the Babe was born and laid in the cratch.'

'We shall never get her to dream our dreams if we let her stay there on the doorstep,' cried the Piskeys, looking strangely at one another. 'We never had such trouble to make a cheeld dream our dreams before.'

'Dream your poor old Grannie feels the cold from the open door,' said a Dinky Man, jumping on to Phillida's nose with all his weight, which caused her to jerk her head in her sleep, and made the Dinky Man lose his balance, and over he toppled on the heads of his tiny companions sitting at the bottom of the pillow near the child's soft white neck, much to the amusement of the other Piskeys and his own. They laughed so much, including the wee fellow who was heavy-heeled, that he could not order the dream, and a Piskey, when he could stop laughing for a minute, jumped up and stepped on to

Phillida's nose, and as he passed over its bridge he said:

'Dream that you shut the door on the cold and the Sky Goose's feathers, and come back to the table.' And Phillida reluctantly dreamt as the Dinky Man ordered, and in her dream she saw herself sitting at the table facing her grandmother, who was munching a bit of the cake and smacking her withered old lips.

'This is a lovely cake, cheeld-vean.* We must eat every crumb of it, for we shall never have such another.'

Phillida was glad her Grannie liked the cake, and she began to eat the generous slice the old woman had given her, and as she ate it she thought it was so delicious that she must go on eating cake for ever and ever. 'I shan't want to eat grail-bread after this,' she said, laughing out loud in her sleep. 'I shall always eat cake made

'" Of fairy cow's cream
And every good thing."'

She was enjoying her dream-cake so very very much in her sleep that the Dinky Men would have liked her to go on eating it; but the quick ticking of Tamsin's clock told them that time was flying, and they had not yet finished ordering her dreams.

'Dream, little Phillida—dream that you and Grannie Tredinnick have eaten all the cake, and

* Child-little.

The Little Cake-bird

there is nothing left but the little cake-bird,' said one of the Dinky Men passing over the bridge of her nose; 'and that Grannie says the little cake-bird is yours.'

Phillida dreamt all that, and in her dream her grandmother said, in her kind old voice: 'The little bird on the top of the cake belongs to the cheeld of the house, and Phillida is the only cheeld in my little house. Take the cake-bird, Phillida, my dear;' and Phillida took it and held it in her little warm hand.

As she was holding it thus a Piskey stepped lightly as a ladybird on to her nose, and as he passed over its bridge he said:

' Dream, Phillida, dream that your little cake-bird is alive and wants to fly and sing;' and the child dreamt that the little cake-bird was alive, and was fluttering in her little warm hand, and then it flew out of her hand up to the thatch, and began to sing a wonderful song.

' What is my little cake-bird singing?' asked Phillida in her sleep.

' It is singing it is a fairy-bird,' said a Dinky Man, passing over the bridge of her nose, 'and that it is going to sing with other little fairy-birds in the Dinky People's land.'

' I don't think my little cake-bird is singing it is a fairy-bird and going to sing in the Dinky People's country,' said the child in her sleep. ' Its song is much too happy and beautiful for that. What *is* it singing? Please tell me. I do want to know. Can't you tell me?' she asked as the Piskeys looked at one another. 'Ah! I know now what its song is about. My little cake-bird is singing a little song because it is a little Christmas bird, and was on top of a Christmas cake! Isn't it a lovely song? It has changed its tune now, and it is singing a golden song about the Babe who was born on Christmas Day in the morning. I am a little Christian cheeld and know! Listen, listen!' she cried, clasping her hands and lifting her sweet child-face to the thatch. 'Isn't it wonderful? It thinks it is a little golden bird, and one day will sing with the Great White Angel Birds Grannie told me about.'

'Somebody far greater than we little Piskeys is ordering Phillida's dreams,' said the Dinky Men one to another, 'which are much more beautiful than we can order.'

Just then old Tamsin's clock struck the midnight hour, and the Piskeys got off the bed, went across the room, climbed up the durn of the door and out through the keyhole on to the moors, and in a little while they were hastening over the snow-covered turf to the Piskey Circle, which was a big round door to the Dinky People's land under the moors.

The Impounded Crows

20161

THE NEW YORK
PUBLIC LIBRARY

ASTOR, LENOX AND
TILDEN FOUNDATIONS.

The Impounded Crows

A SMALL boy called Jim Nancarrow was sitting one day eating a pasty on top of the Crow Pound, a large enclosure built on a common by the far-famed St. Neot to impound the pilfering crows of the parish that bears his name.

Jim was the son of a thatcher, and he was waiting to accompany his father to a distant hamlet to help him to thatch a cottage. He looked a nice little lad in his clean white smock and nankeen breeches and soft felt hat—much the worse for wear—shading his bright young face and clear blue eyes.

As he was waiting for his father and eating his pasty, which his mother had given him for his dinner, he saw a crow flying over Goonzion Downs, of which the Crow Pound common was a part.

As he watched it he thought of the pilfering crows which, according to the old tale, little St. Neot impounded there from morning till evening on Sundays, that his people might go to church undisturbed by fear of the great black thievish birds which ate up the corn sown in their fields. Jim had often heard this story from the old people of the parish, and whenever he saw a crow he wondered if it were a relation of the wicked crows their patron Saint had impounded.

The crow that the boy was watching was flying in the direction of the Crow Pound, and when it came near it alighted on the top of the wall quite close to the lad.

The crow was lean to look at, and scanty of feathers, and such a sorry-looking bird that Jim broke off a piece of his pasty and threw to him, which he ate as if he were starving.

'One would think you were one of the pilfering crows of St. Neot's time,' said Jim, tossing him another piece of his pasty; and to his surprise, the bird answered back:

'I am!'

'Are you?' cried Jim, staring hard at the crow. 'Well, you look ancient enough to be one of those birds, though I have always understood that our patron Saint lived ever so long ago, when Alfred the Great was a little chap like me. But p'r'aps crows tell lies as well as pilfer.'

'If I am not one of the identical crows St. Neot was unkind enough to put into this pound,' croaked the big black bird, eyeing Jim and his pasty with his bright little eye, 'I am a descendant of theirs in the direct line. I truly am,' as the lad stared as if he did not believe the assertion. 'Those poor impounded crows learnt the language of men during the long hours of their imprisonment, listening to all the little Saint and his people said about them outside this pound, and they passed on their dearly-bought knowledge to their children through long generations.'

'Then you are quite "high learnt," as the old Granfer men say,' cried Jim, gazing up at the bird in open-eyed amazement.

'I confess I am,' returned the crow with due modesty, 'especially in the old Cornish tongue, in which I can swear to any extent. I am not going to use bad language now,' as Jim took up a stone to throw at him. 'You would not understand it if I did. I am also "high learnt" in the needs of the body, and I shall be ever so grateful for a bit more of your pasty. It isn't nice to have an aching void inside one's little feather stumjacket.'

'I suppose it can't be,' said the lad, dropping the stone and breaking off a large piece of his pasty to toss to the bird.

He was a feeling-hearted little fellow, and the crow's quaint appeal touched him, and the sorry-looking bird, with his bedraggled tail, had most of his pasty.

'I have had a good meal for once in my life, and am full fed,' said the crow, when the last of the pasty was eaten; and he perched on a stone, starred with stonecrop, and fluffed out all the feathers he possessed, and looked with a comical expression at Jim.

'I am better fed than little St. Neot after his poor little meal of fish,' he continued, still eyeing the boy,

103

'and I am feeling so comfortable that I am inclined for a chat.'

'Are you?' cried Jim, who thought this great black crow was a wonderful crow, which he certainly was. 'I don't know what to yarn about.'

'I do, then,' answered the bird quickly. 'I suppose you have heard the old whiddle* how the little St. Neot put the poor crows into this pound.'

'Yes, I have heard about it from the Granfer men and Grannie women here at Churchtown,' said Jim, turning his face towards a little village close to the church which he could just see from where he was sitting. 'But they never made much of a story of it.'

'Didn't they? Then perhaps you would like to hear the crows' version of the old tale,' said the crow. 'It will tell you that their morals were not so black as the farmers in this parish made out to the Holy Man.'

'I don't mind, if you are quick about it,' said Jim. 'I am going to a farm with my father to help him do some thatching when he has finished his dinner.'

'I cannot be driven after such a heavy meal of pasty,' croaked the crow; 'and if I may not take my time, I won't tell it at all.'

'As you like,' cried Jim with fine indifference; but the bird was anxious to tell the whiddle, and he began:

'We crows always considered it within our right to take what we could,' said the crow, 'and pilfering,

* Tale.

104

'Perhaps you would like to hear the crows' version of the tale?'

The Impounded Crows

as the farmers hereabouts were pleased to call it, was the only way the crows had of picking up a living, and they watched their opportunity to take what they needed to satisfy their hunger when the farmers were not about. But back in those far-away days when St. Neot dwelt here to try and make people good, times were dreadfully bad, especially for crows. The people were all tillers of the land in those days, and lived by the sweat of their brow, as crows did by pilfering. There was no other way open to them, and the farmers had their eyes on the land and on us poor hungry birds from dawn to dark, except on the Rest Day; and the only chance the crows had of filling their stomachs was on Sunday, when the people went to church.

'The starving crows looked forward to Sunday as only poor starving birds with empty crops could, and the moment one of the elder crows gave the signal, which he did in the crow way, they all flew off to the corn-sown fields, and had a regular feast. My word! and didn't they feed! They picked out with their sharp beaks every grain of corn they could find.

'When the farmers found out the hungry crows had eaten up all the corn they had sown, there was the Black Man to pay, and the poor crows were anathematized from one end of the parish to the other.

'The farmers resowed their fields, but they took good care to watch and see that the crows did not rob them of their toil; and they were always about the corn-sown land, Sundays as well as week-days, and the crows had to go supperless to bed, and little St. Neot had to preach to bare walls.

'The Saint was greatly distressed at his people's neglect of their religious duties, and he told them how wicked it was to stay away from church. The people said they were sorry, but declared it was the fault of the pilfering crows.

'"The pilfering crows!" cried the Holy Man. "What have the crows to do with your stopping away from the House of God?"

'"Everything," answered the farmers; and they told little St. Neot that whenever they sowed bread-corn in their fields the wicked crows came and ate it all up, and that if he could not prevent them from doing this wickedness, they must keep away from church and watch their fields. "We and our children must have bread to eat," they added, which was true enough—true for crows as well as men.

'The Holy Man was very much grieved to hear the cause of their not coming to church, and he said he would devise some means to prevent the crows from robbing the fields whilst they were attending to their worship.

'St. Neot was as good as his word, and it was noised about in the parish that he was building a great square enclosure of moorstone and mould about half a mile from the church; and when it was finished, he told his wondering people it was a pound for crows, which he meant to impound on Sundays from dawn till dusk, so that the farmers might come to church and worship without having their minds disturbed by fear of those black little robbers eating their corn.

'There was a fearful to-do among the poor hungry crows when they learned what St. Neot had done; and although they knew they were within their right to steal when they were hungry—and they were always hungry, poor things!—they were sorry they ate up the corn the farmers had sown, and every crow looked forward to the coming Rest Day with fear and trembling.

'Well, Sunday came, as Sundays will,' continued the crow, 'and before the sun had risen little St. Neot made known his will to the crows that they were to come to be impounded, and such power had the Saint over beast and bird that the crows had no choice save to obey, and long before St. Neot's bell rang out to call his people to worship in the little church which he had built for them by the aid of his two-deer team and one-hare team, all the crows in the parish came as they were bidden to be impounded in the Crow Pound.

'And, my gracious! what a lot of them came! There were crows of all sorts and conditions, all ages and sizes! There were great-great-great Granfer and Grannie Crows! there were great-great Granfer and Grannie Crows! great Granfer and Grannie

Crows by the score! Grannie Crows by the hundred! Mammie and Daddy Crows by the thousand! and as for the children, and great-great-grand-children, they could hardly be counted! Even poor little Baby Crows, just able to fly, were there!

'The Crow Pound was chock-full of crows, and all the place was as black as St. Neot's gown. And as for the noise they made, it was enough to turn the Holy Man's brain; but it didn't.

'The little Saint did not expect to see so many crows, it was certain, though he expected a goodly number, by the big enclosure he had made; and the old tale says that, when he saw so many birds, he exclaimed with uplifted hands, "My goodness! what a lot of crows!" and he looked round at this great assemblage—all in respectable black—in open-eyed amazement.

'The people who came flocking to church when they heard that the crows were safe in the Crow Pound were almost as astonished as St. Neot to see such a big congregation of birds.

'The church was too far away from the pound for the crows to hear the little Saint preaching, but when the wind blew up from Churchtown they could hear the singing, and to show you they were not so bad as the farmers made out to the Holy Man, they croaked as loud as ever they could when Mass was sung, and were as silent as the grave during the time St. Neot was preaching.

'Every year, from sowing time till the corn was

The Impounded Crows

reaped and safe in the barn, the crows were impounded every Sunday from the early morning till
evening whilst little St. Neot lived.'

      *   *   *   *   *

'Is that all?' asked Jim, who listened to the
crow's version of the old tale till it was finished.

'Yes,' answered the great black bird with a croak,
and when he had said that he took to his wings and
flew away as fast as he could fly over Goonzion
Downs, the way he had come.

'That wisht-looking crow did not tell the old
whiddle half bad,' said Jim to himself, as he
watched the bird fly away. 'Shouldn't I like to
have seen this old pound full of crows! It must
have been terribly funny when St. Neot looked in
upon them and cried, "My goodness! what a lot of
crows!" It must have been as good as a Christmas
play. There, father is coming. That sharp-eyed
old crow must have seen him climbing the hill.'

The Piskeys' Revenge

The Piskeys' Revenge

ONCE upon a time, so the old story begins, there were an old man and his wife called Granfer and Grannie Nankivell, who lived on a moor, and a small grand-daughter who lived with them.

Genefer was the name of this little girl. She was a small brown child. Brown as a Piskey, her grandfather said; but, brown as she was, she was exceedingly pretty. Her lips were as red as the reddest of berries, and the glow on her cheeks matched her lips.

Her grandfather was a turf-cutter, and most of his days had been spent cutting turf on the Cornish moors.

When this old man was between sixty and seventy he cleared out a whole bog, which happened to be a Piskey-bed.

The Piskeys never like their sleeping-places to be disturbed, and when they found out Granfer Nankivell had done it, they were very angry, and set up Piskey-lights to lead him astray when he came home. But they did it in vain as far as he was concerned. The old turf-cutter was very learned in Piskeys' wiles, and never ventured across the moors without wearing one of his garments inside out, and this made him Piskey-proof, which means that the Piskeys had no power to harm him or to lead him out of his way.

But the sly Little People knew a thing or two as well as Granfer Nankivell, and when they found out that their Piskey-lights failed, they set their sharp little wits to work to do him harm in some other way.

After much watching they discovered that the old turf-cutter had a weakness for sweet things, and that the greatest treat his wife could give him was sugar biscuits of her own making and a big plate of junket. They also found out that Grannie Nankivell, whenever she made these delicacies, put them over-night into her spence* for safety.

They made up their minds that they would punish the old turf-cutter for taking away their nice soft green Piskey-bed by doing him out of his junket and biscuits, and they told some distant relations of theirs, the Fairy Moormen, to keep an eye upon the spence-window, and whenever they saw Grannie Nankivell bring a bowl of junket and a dish of biscuits into her spence, they must come with all speed and tell them.

' We'll watch too,' they said; ' but in case we are away dancing or setting up Piskey-lights, you must watch for us,' which the Tiny Moormen were quite pleased to do.

* A small storeroom for victuals.

The Piskeys' Revenge

But the moor fairies watched in vain for many a week, and just as they were beginning to fear that Grannie Nankivell was never going to make any more biscuits and junket for her husband, she set to and made some, and when they were made she took them into the spence, as she always did.

The spence opened out from the kitchen, and was quite a little room in itself, with a tiny window facing the moors. In front of the window was a stone bench, and near it a square oak table.

The Tiny Moormen were peeping in at the window when the old woman put the bowl of junket on the table and the dish of sugar biscuits on the bench, and the moment her back was turned they tore off to the Piskeys with the news.

'A big round basin full of lovely cool junket,' they cried, 'and a dish heaping full of round biscuits, yellow and white with eggs and sugar, with which they are made. I heard the old woman say that she had never made better, and all for Granfer Nankivell, 'cause 'tis his birthday to-morrow.'

'Birthday or no birthday, Granfer Nankivell shan't taste one,' cried the little Piskeys. 'No fy, he shan't! He turned us out of our beds, and we'll do him out of his biscuits and junket, see if we won't!'

'That's right!' said the Fairy Moormen, who were hand and glove with the Piskeys, 'only please save some for us.'

They and the Piskeys hastened away to the turf-cutter's cottage, and when the turf-cutter and his

The Piskeys got in and ate up the bowl of junket, and passed out the biscuits.

wife had gone to bed, the Piskeys got into the spence and ate up the big bowl of junket, and passed out the biscuits to the Tiny Moormen.

The Piskeys' Revenge

When Grannie Nankivell went to her spence the next day she found the junket-bowl empty and every biscuit gone.

She said she could not imagine who had taken the things, but looked suspiciously at her little grand-daughter Genefer.

'The cat must have got into the spence and done me out of my birthday treat,' said the old turf-cutter. 'You must shut the spence-window the next time you put a junket in there.'

'But the biscuits have gone as well as the junket,' said the old woman, still looking at little Genefer. 'Cats have no liking for sugar biscuits, that ever I heard tell of.'

The next time Grannie Nankivell took biscuits and a junket into her spence she shut the window and also the door; but when she got up the following morning and went to see if they were safe, lo and behold! the junket-bowl was again empty and the biscuits were gone.

''Tis a two-legged cat who has eaten up my beautiful biscuits and junket,' she said to her husband; and she turned and looked at little Genefer.

'I am not the two-legged cat who ate up all the nice things you made for Granfer,' cried the child, meeting the old woman's glance with her honest brown eyes.

'I never said you did,' said Grannie Nankivell; 'but 'tis queer the junket-bowl is empty and every biscuit gone from the dish.'

'I expect it was a dog which got into the spence and licked up the junket and ate the biscuits,' put in the old turf-cutter. 'I would lock and bar the spence-door, if I were you, the next time I put such nice things in there.'

'I will,' she said.

The next time Grannie Nankivell made biscuits and a junket she barred the window of the spence and locked the door, and the next morning, before Genefer dressed, she went to see if her junket and biscuits were all right; but the little round biscuits, which she had so carefully made and sugared, were every one gone, and the junket-bowl was quite empty, and as dry as a bone.

''Tis our little grandcheeld who has eaten it all!' cried Grannie Nankivell in great anger to the old turf-cutter. 'No cat or dog could get into a spence with door locked and window barred.'

'I don't believe it was Genefer,' said the old man stoutly.

'If it was not Genefer, who was it, pray? Biscuits and junkets don't eat up themselves, any more than dogs and cats can get through keyholes and barred windows.'

'That's true,' said Granfer Nankivell; 'all the same, I am certain sure that our dear little grand-cheeld would not go and eat up the things.'

'Then who did?' asked the old woman with a snap.

'The little Piskeys, I shouldn't wonder,' he

answered. ' My great-grannie told me they were little greedy-guts, and in her days they used to skim the cream off the milk, and eat all the cheese-cakes she used to make, unless she put some for them outside on the doorstep. Regular little thieves the Piskeys were in her days. P'raps they haven't learnt to be honest yet. There are plenty about now, and Little Moormen too, by the teheeing and tehoing I have heard lately, waiting, I dare say, to play some of their pranks on me.'

But Grannie Nankivell was still unconvinced, and still believed it was Genefer, and *not* the Piskeys, who ate her biscuits and junket.

One evening the old woman put another bowl of junket and a dish of biscuits in the spence, and was as careful as before to bar the window and lock the door; and in the middle of the night, when her husband was fast asleep and snoring, she got up and came downstairs to see if she could find out for certain who it was that ate up her good things. When she came down, whom should she see but her little grand-daughter Genefer standing by the spence-door in her little bedgown.

' I am fine and glad you have come, Grannie,' whispered the child, before the old woman could say anything. ' I believe it is the Piskeys who have eaten the junket and things you made for Granfer. I saw a dinky little fellow not much bigger than your thumb go in through the keyhole just now. They are having a fine time in there, anyhow,' as her grandmother looked at her oddly. ' If I were you, I would look through the keyhole and see what they are doing.'

And through the keyhole the old woman looked, and saw, to her amazement, scores and scores of green-coated little men, whiskered like a man, on the oak table, standing round the junket-bowl ladling out the rich, thick junket with their tiny little hands, and half a dozen other little chaps were up in the window-sill passing out her delicious sugar biscuits to the Tiny Moormen, who were even more whiskered and bearded than their distant relations, the Piskeys.

By their faces, they were all greatly enjoying themselves, and at the expense of Granfer Nankivell, the turf-cutter !

Grannie Nankivell was so astonished that she lost her mouth-speech,* but when she found it her old voice shrilled through the keyhole :

' Filling your little bellies with the junket and biskeys I made for my old man, be 'ee ?' she cried. ' I'll wring the necks of every one of you—iss fy, I will !'

The old woman spoke too soon to carry out her threat, for she had no sooner spoken than the Piskeys vanished, the Tiny Moormen as well, and where they went she never knew.

But her husband told her the little rascals were still in the spence when she could not see them.

' They have the power to make themselves visible

* Power of utterance.

The Piskeys' Revenge

or invisible, whichever is most convenient to them,'
he said.

'They have done you out of your biscuits and
junket a good many times, anyhow,' cried the old
woman.

'Iss,' said Granfer Nankivell, 'they have; and as
I did away with the Piskey-beds, we are quits. I
only hope they will be of the same mind, and won't
come any more and eat up those nice things you
make for me. I am quite longing for a plateful of
junket and one of your sweet biscuits.'

Whether the Piskeys thought the old turf-cutter
was sufficiently punished for clearing out their sleeping-places, or whether Grannie Nankivell's threat
to wring their necks frightened them away, we
cannot tell. At all events, they and the Tiny Moormen kept away from the cottage on the moor, and
whenever the old woman made sugar biscuits and
sweet junket, and put them in the spence, no two-
legged cat, Moormen or Piskeys, ever ate up those
specially-made dainties; and little Genefer's honesty
was never again doubted.

The Old Sky Woman

The Old Sky Woman

WHEN winter brought the cold north wind, and the snowflakes began to fall, the little North Cornwall children were always told that the Old Woman was up in the sky plucking her Goose.

The children were very interested in the Old Sky Woman and her great White Goose, and they said, as they lifted their soft little faces to the grey of the cloud and watched the feathers of the big Sky Goose come whirling down, that she was a wonderful woman and her Goose a very big Goose.

'I want to climb up to the sky to see the Old Woman plucking her Goose,' cried a tiny boy; and he asked his mother to show him the great Sky Stairs. But his mother could not, for she did not know where the Sky Stairs were; so the poor little boy could not go up to see the Old Sky Woman plucking the beautiful feathers out of her big White Goose.

'Where does the Old Woman keep her great White Goose?' asked another child, with eyes and hair as dark as a raven's wing, as he watched the snow-white feathers come dancing down.

'In the beautiful Sky Meadows behind the clouds,' his mother said.

North Cornwall Fairies

'What is the Old Sky Woman going to do with her great big Goose when she has picked her bare?' queried a little maid with sweet, anxious eyes.

'Stuff it with onions and sage,' her Granfer said.

'The Old Sky Woman sweeping out the Sky Goose's house.'

'What will she do then with her great big Goose?' the little maid asked.

'Hang it up on the great Sky Goose-jack and roast for her Christmas dinner,' her Granfer said.

'Poor old Goose!' cried the little maid.

'I don't believe the Old Sky Woman would be so

unkind as to kill and pluck her great big Goose,' said a wise little maid with sunny hair and eyes as blue as the summer sea. 'Winter-time is the Sky Goose's moulting time, and the Old Sky Woman is sweeping out the Sky Goose's house with her great Sky Broom, and the White Goose's feathers are flying down to keep the dear little flowers nice and warm till the north wind has gone away from the Cornish Land.'

'Perhaps that is so, dear little maid,' her Granfer said.

Reefy, Reefy Rum

Reefy, Reefy Rum

A SMALL girl called Nancy Parnell came down from Wadebridge to Padstow one St. Martin's summer to stay with her Grannie.

The Grannie was old and weak in her legs, and could not take her granddaughter out to see the sights of the little old-world town, with its narrow streets and ancient houses, so the child had to go by herself.

When she had seen all there was to be seen in the town, she went up to look at the church, of which she had heard from her mother, who was a Padstow woman, and the quaint little figures on the buttresses of the south wall.

It was between the lights when she got there, bu she could see the carved figures quite distinctly, which were a lion with its mouth wide open, a unicorn with a crown encircling its neck, and a young knight, standing between them, holding a shield ; and when she had taken them all in she repeated a funny old rhyme which her mother told her she used to say when she was a little maid and lived at Padstow.   The rhyme was as follows :

'Reefy, reefy rum,
  Without teeth or tongue ;
  If you'll have me,
  Now I am a-come.'

North Cornwall Fairies

The rhyme—a taunt and an invitation in one—
was very rude, and so was the little girl who repeated
it; but the lion, the unicorn, and the little knight
did not take any notice of her, and looked straight
before them as they had done ever since they were
carved on the wall. But Nancy was somewhat
afraid of the effect of the rhyme on those quaint
little figures, especially on the open-mouthed lion,
who had no sign of teeth or tongue; and she ran
round the great square-turreted tower, and took
refuge under the pentice roof of the gateway, and
sat on the bench to see if they would leave their
stations on the wall and come after her; but they
did not.

The little stone knight and the two animals had a
strange fascination for the little Wadebridger, and
the next evening again found her in the beautiful
churchyard gazing up at them with her bright child-
eyes, and as she gazed she repeated the same rude
rhyme :

> ' Reefy, reefy rum,
> Without teeth or tongue ;
> If you'll have me,
> Now I am a-come.'

But they took not the smallest notice of her, nor of
her rhyme, and the young knight did not lift as much
as an eyelash ; but the child, now the rhyme was
said, was even more apprehensive than ever of the
effect it might have, and ran round the tower and
again took refuge in the old gateway, and waited to

She took to her heels and ran for her life.

THE NEW YORK
PUBLIC LIBRARY

ASTOR, LENOX AND
TILDEN FOUNDATIONS,
C ⌐   L

see if they would come down from the wall and try
to catch her; but they never came.

The last evening of her stay at Padstow, Nancy
went once more to the churchyard to have another
look at the figures, and to taunt them with having
no teeth or tongue.

It was not quite so late as the first two evenings
she had come thither, and the robins were singing
their evensong in the churchyard trees.

As she stood staring up at the figures, a shaft of
light from the sun setting between the trees fell across
their faces, and the eyes of the little knight seemed to
look down in sad reproach at the rude little maid as
she again repeated the rhyme which was even ruder
than she knew.

Her voice was shrill and loud, and was heard above
the robins' cheerful song.

She had hardly finished the rhyme when she saw
the lion move from his place on the wall, followed
by the unicorn and the young knight, and come
sliding down. She did not wait to see them reach
the bottom, for she took to her heels and ran for her
life; but she could hear the figures carved in stone
coming after her as she flew round the tower, and
her heart was beating faster than the church clock
when she reached the gateway.

The gate, fortunately for her, was open wide, and
she caught hold of it, and banged it behind her as
the lion with his gaping mouth came up to it.

She looked over her shoulder as she turned to run

down the street, and she saw the three figures all in a row—the young knight in the middle holding his shield—gazing at her through the round wooden bars of the gate. The lion looked savage, and but for the brave little knight with his pure young face, who seemed to have a restraining power upon both animals, he might have broken the bars and come through the gate and made small bones of the child who had invited them three times to come down and have her !

The little Wadebridger ran back to her Grannie, and told her about the rhyme she had said to the little stone figures on the wall of Padstow Church, and how they had come down and run after her to the gate. Her good old Grannie said it would have served her right if they had broken the gate and got her. 'A lesson to you, my dear,' she cried, ' never to be rude to man or beast, especially to figures carved on church walls.'

The three little stone figures stood all in a row on the gate step till the child was out of sight, and finding she did not return, they went back to their places on the buttresses of the grey old church, and there they are still; and, as far as we know, they have never left them since Nancy Parnell, the little Wade-bridger, repeated ' Reefy, reefy rum ' three times, and that was when our great-great-grandmothers were children.

The Little Horses and Horsemen of Padstow

The Little Horses and Horsemen of Padstow

A T the bottom of the same old town there is a house which has two tiny little men on horseback on the top of its roof. They have stood there for hundreds of years, and they never leave their places save when they hear the great church clock strike the hour of midnight, when, it is said, they leave the red tiles, and gallop round the market-place and through the streets of the little town.

These gallant little horsemen have seen the house on which they stand almost rebuilt—changed from an old-world building with quaint windows and doors

into quite a modern one—and they have the sorrow
of knowing that the only things left that are ancient
are the walls, the red tile-ridge, their little horses,
and themselves.

Long generations of Padstow children have seen
these quaint little men on horseback, and many a
question have they asked concerning them ; but the
only thing they ever learnt was that whenever they
hear the church clock strike twelve in the middle of
the night they come down from the roof, gallop
round the market, and through the streets, as we
have just said.   But as children are generally in bed
at that late hour, none were ever fortunate enough
to see them do this wonderful feat, except little Robin
Curgenven, the son of a toymaker, and it happened
in this way:

One evening when Robin was about nine years
old his father and mother went to a party; and as it
was a party only for grown-up people, they left him
at home asleep in bed.

Robin slept sound as a ringer till just before
twelve, when he awoke, and finding he was alone in
the house, he crept out of bed, opened the front door,
which was under the roof, and went out and stood
on the top of an external stone stairway which led
down to the market-place.

The house where he lived was as quaint and old
as the one on which the little men rode so gallantly,
and it faced it.   As he stood at the head of the steps
the church clock began to strike the hour of mid-

night. It had only struck four or five when he remembered what he had heard about those wonderful little horsemen and their steeds, and he looked across the market to see if what he had been told about them was really true.

He could see the house quite plainly, and the little horses and horsemen, for it was a clear night and full moon.

The moment the clock had done striking Robin saw to his great delight the two little men on their two little horses leave the housetop and leap into the street, and go galloping round and round the market-place as his parents assured him they did when they heard the clock strike twelve.

The little horses galloped so funnily, and the tiny riders sat so bolt upright on their quaint little steeds, that Robin laughed to see them, and said they looked exactly like the wooden toy horses and horsemen in his father's shop. And as they went galloping, galloping that queer little gallop, he clapped his hands and cheered like a Cornishman.

The tiny little horsemen took no notice of the excited boy on the top of the stairs, and the moment they had finished their gallop round the old market they came through the narrow opening at the foot of the stairs, and galloped away up the street as fast as they could.

So excited was little Robin Curgenven when he saw the tiny horsemen gallop away that he flew down the steps and tore after them, quite forgetting that his feet were bare, and that he had nothing on save his little white nightshirt.

He ran very fast; but fast as he ran, he could not overtake those swift little horses, and by the time he got to the bottom of Middle Street they were nearly at the top.

When they reached the head of that street the tiny horsemen pulled up their horses for a minute outside an ancient-looking house with a porch-room set on wooden pillars, and then they turned up Workhouse Hill and disappeared.

Robin ran faster than before, and the tails of his little nightshirt flew out behind him on the wind as he ran; and he never stopped running till he was half-way up Church Street, when he saw the little horses and their riders galloping down towards him.

They had been to the head of the town, and were returning; and he got on the footpath and stood near an arched passage, and waited for them to pass.

He did not have to wait long, and so fast did they come you would have thought they were galloping for a wager. They seemed to be enjoying their gallop through the streets of the sleeping old town amazingly; and Robin, as he fixed his bright young eyes upon them, saw, or thought he saw, a broad grin on their queer little faces as they galloped by.

The barefooted little lad, in his little night-garment, ran beside the quaint little horses and the little horsemen for a short distance, but they galloped

They galloped much faster than he could run.

THE NEW YORK
PUBLIC LIBRARY

ASTOR, LENOX AND
TILDEN FOUNDATIONS

much faster than he could run, and soon outdistanced him; and, run as hard as ever he could, he could not overtake them, but he heard the ringing of the tiny horses' hoofs on the hard road as they went galloping down through the town.

When he reached the bottom of the town and the house where the little men and their horses usually stood, he glanced up, and to his surprise saw them standing on the tile-ridge, looking as if they had never left it.

Robin gazed at them till he began to feel cold, and then he went back across the market to his own house; and half an hour later, when his father and mother came home from the party, they found him fast asleep on one of the steps with his toes tucked up under him.

' The funny little horses and little horsemen did hear the clock strike twelve, and galloped round the market and through the town same as you told me,' said Robin in a sleepy voice, when his father picked him up and carried him into the house. ' I saw them with my own eyes, and I ran after them up as far as Church Street. They galloped so funnily and so fast; I am glad I saw them.'

' So am I,' said his father, laughing, thinking his small son had dreamt it as he lay asleep on the step. ' You are the first little chap who ever saw them come down from the roof and gallop, and I fancy you will be the last.'

Little Robin Curgenven may have been the first

North Cornwall Fairies

to see them gallop as his father said, but he may not be the last, for the quaint little horses and horsemen are still on the roof of the house, and it is told that they still gallop through Padstow streets, and round what once was the market, when they hear the church clock strike twelve!

How Jan Brewer was Piskey-
laden

How Jan Brewer was Piskey-laden

THE moon was near her setting as a tall, broad-shouldered man called Jan Brewer was walking home to Constantine Bay to his cottage on the edge of a cliff.

He was singing an old song to himself as he went along, and he sang till he drew near the ruins of Constantine Church, standing on a sandy common near the bay. As he grew near the remains of this ancient church, which were clearly seen in the moonshine, he thought he heard someone laughing, but he was not quite sure, for the sea was roaring on the beach below the common, and the waves were making a loud noise as they dashed up the great headland of Trevose.

'I was mistaken; 'twas nobody laughing,' said Jan to himself, and he walked on again, singing as before; and he sang till he came near a gate, which opened into a field leading to his cottage, but when he got there he could not see the gate or the gateway.

'I was so taken up with singing the old song, that I must have missed my way,' he said again to himself. 'I'll go back to the head of the common and start afresh,' which he did; and when he got to the place where his gate ought to have been, he could not find it to save his life.

'I must be clean mazed,'* he cried. 'I have never got out of my reckoning before, nor missed finding my way to our gate, even when the night has been as dark as pitch. It isn't at all dark to-night; I can see Trevose Head'—looking across the bay—'and yet I can't see my own little gate! But I en't a-going to be done; I'll go round and round this common till I *do* find my gate.'

And round and round the common he went, but find his gate he could not.

Every time he passed the ruins of the church a laugh came up from the pool below the ruins, and once he thought he saw a dancing light on the edge of the pool, where a lot of reeds and rushes were growing.

'The Little Man in the Lantern is about to-night,' he said to himself, as he glanced at the pool. 'But I never knew he was given to laughing before.'

Once more he went round the common, and when he had passed the ruins he heard giggling and laughing, this time quite close to him; and looking down on the grass, he saw to his astonishment hundreds of Little Men and Little Women with tiny lights in their hands, which they were flinking † about as they laughed and giggled.

The Little Men wore stocking-caps, the colour of ripe briar berries, and grass-green coats, and the

* Mad.   † Waving.

Ruins of Constantine Church.

THE NEW YORK
PUBLIC LIBRARY

ASTOR, LENOX AND
TILDEN FOUNDATIONS.

How Jan Brewer was Piskey-laden

Little Women had on old grandmother cloaks of the same vivid hue as the Wee Men's coats, and they also wore fascinating little scarlet hoods.

' I believe the great big chap sees us,' said one of the Little Men, catching sight of Jan's astonished face. 'He must be Piskey-eyed, and we did not know it.'

' Is he really?' cried one of the Dinky* Women. ' 'Tis a pity,' as the Little Man nodded. ' But we'll have our game over him all the same.'

' That we will,' cried all the Little Men and Little Women in one voice ; and, forming a ring round the great tall fellow, they began to dance round him, laughing, giggling, tehoing, and flashing up their lights as they danced.

They went round him so fast that poor Jan was quite bewildered, and whichever way he looked there were these Little Men and Little Women giggling up into his bearded face. And when he tried to break through their ring they went before him and behind him, making a game over him, he said !

He was at their mercy and they knew it ; and when they saw the great fellow's misery, they only laughed and giggled the more.

' We've got him !' they cried to each other, and they said it with such gusto and with such a comical expression on their tiny brown faces, that Jan, bewildered as he was, and tired with going round the common so many times, could not help laughing,

* Little.

155

they looked so very funny, particularly when the Little Women winked up at him from under their little scarlet hoods.

The Piskeys—for they were Piskeys—hurried him down the common, dancing round him all the time; and when he got there he felt so mizzy-mazey with those tiny whirling figures going round and round him like a whirligig, that he did not know whether he was standing on his head or his heels. He was also in a bath of perspiration—' sweating leaking,' he expressed it—and, putting his hand in his pocket to take out a handkerchief to mop his face, he remembered having been told that, if ever he got Piskey-laden, he must turn his coat pockets inside out, when he would be free at once from his Piskey tormentors. He immediately acted on this suggestion, and in a minute or less his coat-pockets were hanging out, and all the Little Men and the Little Women had vanished, and there, right in front of him, he saw his own gate! He lost no time in opening it, and in a very short time was in his thatched cottage on the cliff.

They began to dance round him.

The Small People's Fair

The Small People's Fair

I N the same parish where Jan Brewer was Piskey-
laden on Constantine Common there is a beautiful lane called Tresallyn. It has high mossy
hedges, where ferns grow in abundance, and where
speedwells love to display their multitude of blue
blossoms.

This lane is said to be a regular Piskeys' haunt,
where all the Wee Folk in the neighbourhood meet.
People who have passed through this lane in the
evening or late at night have heard the Piskeys
laughing; but nobody, as far as we know, except one
young fellow, ever had the good fortune to see them,
and he, like Jan Brewer, had the gift of seeing what
others could not.

Hender Bennett was the name of this young fellow,
and he lived at a farm near Tresallyn Lane. One
night, after he had been over to Towan, a village
about a mile and a half away, to see a young girl
whom he was courting, he was returning home
through this beautiful old lane, when he was startled
by a burst of music quite close to him. The music
was so sweet and yet so stirring that he wanted to
dance to the tune. He looked about to see whence the
sound was coming, but he could see nothing unusual.

North Cornwall Fairies

It was a glorious night, and the big moon floated like a silver ball in the cloudless blue of the midnight sky, and shone so brightly that he could even see fronds of the ferns standing out quite clearly from the mossy hedge-banks.

As he was looking around, the music grew louder, sweeter, and more stirring, and sending his gaze down the lane to where the trees arched it, he saw a big crowd of Small People holding a fair.

He had heard of Little People's fairs from his great-grannie, but had never hoped to see one, and he was as glad as a bird that he happened to be going down Tresallyn Lane when they were holding one.

The Wee Folk were holding their fair near a gate about a dozen yards or so from where he was standing. As the moon was just then floating over the gate, he could see all the Little People quite plainly, and what they were doing.

The Little Men and the Little Women were all dressed up to the nines in the way of clothes, and although he could not have described the cut of their coats or the style of their gowns, he knew that all the Little Women were lovely, that dear little faces peeped out of quaint bonnets, that they carried frails in their hands, and that Piskey-purses hung by their sides in the same way that his great-grannie's big cotton purse bag hung under her gown.

There were ever so many little standings or stalls on the grass—one here and one there, like currants in his mother's buns, Hender told himself. Every standing was laid out with all sorts of tempting things pleasing to Small People, on which they gazed with evident delight. They asked the price of this thing and that of the little standing women behind the stalls ; and to see the Little People opening their tiny brown Piskey-purses and taking out their fairy money to pay for their purchases was as good as a play.

But what delighted the young fellow most were the Tiny Fiddlers and Pipers ; and to watch the way the Fiddlers elbowed their fiddle-sticks and fiddled was worth walking twelve miles any night to see, he said, to say nothing of watching the Little Men and the Little Women dancing to the tunes the Fiddlers fiddled and the Pipers piped. It was merrymaking with a vengeance, he told himself, and the fiddling, the piping, and the merrymaking at Summercourt Fair were nothing to it !

The fair itself was held a few feet away from the standings and the merrymaking, and when Hender could turn away his gaze for a few minutes to look at the Little People's Fair Park, he saw a sight he feared he should never see again. There were scores of fairy horses, and as many bullocks and cows, and flocks of sheep and goats, none of them much bigger than those quaint little animals in toy farmyards ; but these were all alive, he could tell, by the prancing of the horses ! The sheep were confined within hurdles. There were pigs there as well, only to Hender's eyes

North Cornwall Fairies

they looked exactly like very large sow-pigs,* all of which were in small stone enclosures. Moving about among the animals were Little Men, who were dressed like farmers, but whether they were farmers or not he could not tell.

It was all so wonderfully interesting to Hender that he stood still like one in a dream, till one of the Little Men in a smart green coat went over to a very pretty Little Lady, who reminded him of his own sweetheart whom he had not very long kissed good-night, and asked her if he might treat her to some fairing, and he took hold of her little hand and led her up to the standing. And when he opened his purse to pay for what he bought for his lady-love Hender had to give vent to his feelings, and he cried out: ' I could not have done it better—no, not even if I had bought a fairing for my own little sweet-heart! No fy! I couldn't.'

The words were no sooner spoken when the Small People's fair vanished, Little People and all, and the only thing left to show that a fair had been held were a dozen sow-pigs in a stone enclosure!

* Wood-lice.

The Piskeys who did Aunt Betsy's Work

The Piskeys who did Aunt Betsy's Work

I N our great-great-grandmothers' days people very seldom went away visiting, and when little Nannie Sando received an invitation from her Aunt Betsy—great-aunt really—who lived quite twenty miles from her home on a lonely moor, near Liskard, there was great excitement in Nannie's home.

Nannie's father did not like the thought of her going away so far from home, and her mother did not like it either, but she said Aunt Betsy was well-to-do, and had a stockingful of gold hidden away somewhere; it would not do for them to offend her by refusing to let the child go. So the invitation was accepted, and Nannie was sent off by coach, and met by her aunt in a donkey-cart in Horn Lane, at Liskard, where the coach put up; and that same evening she reached the little house on the moor.

It was quite a nice little house, with two rooms up and two down, and a large garden behind, sheltered by granite boulders fantastically piled one on top of the other. In front of the house were the moors, which, at the time Nannie came to stay with her aunt, were gorgeous with the bloom of heather and other flowers.

Nice as the house was, and beautiful as the moors were, with their background of Kilmar and other Cornish tors, it was a lonely spot for a child to come and stay at, with only an elderly woman for company. But, then, there was the charm of novelty, and there were delights in the shape of her aunt's donkey and cow, and a big black tom-cat called Tinker, to say nothing of the far-stretching moors, which were so beautiful to look at and run wild on.

When Nannie was leaving to go and stay with Aunt Betsy, her mother, with a view to possessing some of the old lady's golden hoard some day, told her little daughter to be very attentive to her aunt. ' Get up when she does,' she said, ' and help her to do her work, and make yourself very useful ;' and the child said she would.

Nannie, when she was going to bed on the evening of her arrival, remembered her mother's injunction, and said to her aunt :

' Please call me when you get up ; I want to help you to clean up the houseplace.'

But the old woman did not call her grand-niece, and let her stay in bed till breakfast-time ; and when the child came down she found all the work done, and everything clean and shining.

' You never called me, Aunt Betsy,' said Nannie reproachfully. ' Mother did so want me to help you.'

' Did she ?' cried the old woman sharply. ' If your

mother told you to help me, she had a motive for it. I know your mother's little ways!'

'She said you were getting up in years,' said Nannie innocently, 'and that the young should spare the old as much as they could.'

'The dear little Brown Piskeys spare my old legs,' said the old woman, looking at the child. 'They come in and do my work before the world gets up.'

'The Piskeys!' cried the child. 'Who are the Piskeys? I never heard of them before.'

'You must be a very ignorant little girl not to have heard tell of the Piskeys,' cried Aunt Betsy, lifting her hands in surprise. 'They are dear Little People who take strange likes and dislikes to human beings. If they happen to like people very much, they come into their house and do their work for them. They have taken quite a fancy to me, and come into my house every night and clean up the houseplace, polish the candlesticks till they shine like gold, scour the pots and pans, and wash and clean everthing that wants cleaning.'

'How very kind of them!' said Nannie. 'They must be dear Little People. I do wish I could see them doing your work, Aunt Betsy. It would be something to tell father and mother when I go home.'

'I don't expect you will have the good fortune to see the Piskeys,' said the old woman. 'They are little invisible Men and Women, and nobody ever sees them unless they happen to be Piskey-eyed. As you have never heard about these dear Wee

Folk till now, it is quite certain you have not the gift.'

'Are *you* Piskey-eyed, Aunt Betsy?' asked Nannie eagerly.

Her aunt did not answer, and told her little grand-niece to sit up at table and eat her breakfast.

The child was too full of the Little People to eat much breakfast, and the more she thought about them, the more anxious she became to see those dear Wee Folk, who were so very, very kind to her Aunt Betsy.

The next morning Nannie got up ever so early, with the hope of seeing the Piskeys, but, early as it was, Aunt Betsy was down before her. The work was all done, and the table laid for breakfast, as on the previous day.

'The Piskeys came and did it long before I was up,' remarked her aunt, not noticing the child's face of disappointment, glancing round the big kitchen, with its stone-flagged floor, just washed, and looking as blue as the tors, and up at the dresser, with its china looking as if it had been washed in sunshine, it was so sparkling; and as for the tall brass candlesticks on the high mantelpiece, they were dazzling in their brightness.

'It isn't fair that the Little People should come in and do all your work when I wanted to help,' said Nannie.

'I am used to Piskeys, but not to children,' returned the old woman. 'If you really want to do something for me, you shall go out on the moors and pick me a nosegay of wild flowers. It will make the kitchen look nice, and will complete the work of the Piskeys.'

Nannie was willing, as she had nothing to do, and she put on her sun-bonnet to go.

'The clover is in blossom,' said her aunt, as the child was going out at the door, 'and if you happen to find one with four leaves you may perhaps get Piskey-eyed, and if you also find a Wee's Nest* you will have the good fortune to see all the Little People in Cornwall!'

'A Wee's Nest is a thing that is never found,' said Nannie; 'but I'll look for a four-leaved clover till I find it. P'raps you found a four-leaved clover, and that is how you can see the Piskeys,' looking round at her aunt with a smile.

The old woman was not given to answering questions, and she only said that four-leaved clovers were not so easy to find as she imagined.

There was an abundance of flowers everywhere on the moors, and Nannie soon gathered a great big nosegay; but although she looked for a four-leaved clover, she could not find one.

Her aunt was very pleased with the flowers when she took them to her, and told her to put them into an earthenware pot, which she did; and when she had had her dinner, she went on the moors again. Tinker, the great tom-cat, with whom she had already made friends, followed her.

* Mare's nest.

171

North Cornwall Fairies

Nannie stayed out on the moors till it was almost bedtime, searching for a four-leaved clover, but she searched in vain.

The next morning, the child, hearing her aunt dressing, got up and dressed too, and, being young and nimble, she was dressed and down first.

When she got to the kitchen, she heard the clatter of pans and

Nannie went on the moors again, and Tinker followed her.

Piskeys who did Aunt Betsy's Work

a tripping to and fro of tiny feet, and little bursts of laughter came from the big spence at the upper end of the kitchen; but she saw nothing living, except Tinker, cleaning his face in front of the fire, and then she heard a patter of small feet going towards the outer kitchen door, and there was silence.

'You have driven away the Piskeys, you young good-for-nothing!' cried Aunt Betsy, coming into the kitchen, buttoning the sleeve of her gown as she came. 'The Little People don't like to be spied on when they are busy working. You should not have got up so early.'

The old woman seemed as much put out as the Piskeys, and she flew round the kitchen doing the work the Small People had left undone, and would not allow Nannie to help at all, not even to lay the cloth for breakfast.

After breakfast, the child, in order to put her aunt in a better mood, went out on the moors to get another nosegay of wild flowers, and she gathered one of every sort she could find.

As she was picking them, Tinker, the cat, who had followed her again to the moors, put his paw on a clover and mewed; and, fearing a bee had stung him, she looked to see, and quite close to his paw was a white four-leaved clover!

'I shall be able to see the Piskeys now!' said Nannie joyfully; and she and Tinker returned to the house.

North Cornwall Fairies

Aunt Betsy was out at the back looking for a hen who had stolen her nest, and she did not come in till dinner-time.

Nannie amused herself meanwhile in arranging the flowers, and when she had done that to her own satisfaction, she passed the four-leaved clover over her eyes three times, and looked round the kitchen to see what she could see. She saw nothing unusual, but she thought she saw a tiny brown laughing face peeping round the kitchen door.

When Aunt Betsy came in from watching the hen, the child told her she had found the four-leaved clover, thanks to Tinker.

Her aunt looked at her queerly, and asked her to show the clover which she had found; and when she saw that it was a four-leaved one, she only said: 'But you have not yet found the Wee's Nest, and you must not expect to see the dear little Brown Piskeys unless you do.'

Nannie hoped she would, all the same, and this hope made her so excited she could not sleep; and when daylight began to creep into the sky she got up, and without waiting to put on more than her little petticoat, she crept downstairs, holding the four-leaved clover in her hand. When she got to the door of the kitchen, leading into it from the passage, she opened it softly and peeped in; and to her delight she saw scores and scores of Little People, all as busy as bees in a field of clover. Some were sweeping the flagged stones, some were washing the

Piskeys who did Aunt Betsy's Work

cloam* and scouring the pots and pans, some were polishing the candlesticks with a soft leather, and others were in the big spence scrubbing the stone benches and doing it all as keenly† as Aunt Betsy herself, which was most wonderful, she thought, considering how tiny they were. For they were not much bigger than a miller's thumb.‡

It was the Little Women Piskeys who were the busiest workers. The Little Men were less industrious; and when Tinker came into the kitchen, they stopped their work of cleaning the milk-pans to pull his great bushy tail and his whiskers. One little scamp of a Piskey—perhaps unconscious that Nannie was now Piskey-eyed—put his thumb to his nose, after the manner of naughty little boys, and made a face at her.

The Piskeys were a merry little lot, and laughed at their work as if it were all play, which perhaps it was; and one little red-capped Piskey danced a hornpipe on the table as several of his companions were about to lay the cloth for Aunt Betsy's breakfast. They stood on the edge of the table, waiting for him to finish his dance, and as he did not seem inclined to do this, they caught hold of him by his legs and tickled him.

The little Piskey who was being tickled, and those who tickled him, looked so comical that Nannie laughed, which made them stop and look round.

* China. † Well.
‡ A very small bird.

175

North Cornwall Fairies

'There is a little maid watching us from the door!' said one of the Piskeys in a whisper. 'She is Piskey-eyed, the same as Aunt Betsy, and she will be spying upon us now, sure as eggs are eggs. I think we had better forsake this house and go and do work for some other old woman.' And, to Nannie's distress, they went, and ever after Aunt Betsy had to do her own work, which made her so cross that she sent poor Nannie home to her parents at the first opportunity she had ; and when she died, which was not a great while after, she left her little hoard of gold to strangers. Nannie's father said 'twas a great pity, but that his wife was to blame, for if she had not urged their little maid to help the old lady to do her work with the unworthy motive of having some of her gold, Nannie would never have wanted to see the Piskeys doing Aunt Betsy's work.

The Piskeys who Carried
their Beds

The Piskeys who Carried
their Beds

MANY years ago the Piskeys used to dance on
a grassy place on the top of the cliffs overlooking Newtrain Bay in the parish of
Padstow. They danced there so often that the grass
was worn quite bare, and until the cliffs on which
they danced were undermined and broken down by
the rough sea, the marks of their tiny feet were
plainly seen.

An old woman who lived a short distance from
Newtrain Cliffs used to tell people interested in
fairies that she had often seen them dancing there.
'They danced two and two,' she said, 'and so near
the edge of the cliff, you would have thought they
would dance over. But they never did; they were
far too clever for that.'

Jinnie Chapman was the name of this old woman.
She was quite a character in her way, and almost as
interesting as the Small People she loved to talk
about.

She was a little quick woman, with twinkling dark
eyes, and whenever she went over to Newtrain to
watch the Piskeys, she wore a black cottage-bonnet
over her neat jinnie-guick cap, a blue print apron,

and a quaint little black turnover with a wide border of red cones. This turnover she called a ' q ' shawl, because the cones on its border were the shape of q's, she said.

It was the great pleasure of her dull, uneventful life to see the Piskeys dancing, which she was simple enough to believe they did to give her pleasure; and she embraced every opportunity to get to the New-train Cliffs to watch them.

Jinnie had watched the Small People so often that she knew every one of them by sight, and how many there were that danced.

They never took any notice of the little old woman in the cottage-bonnet, the quaint shawl, and blue print apron, watching them dancing near a low stone hedge green and gold with samphire; and they laughed and talked to each other just the same as if she were not present.

They never danced, as far as Jinnie knew, except when the moon was high, and they left off dancing when the moon set like a ball of fire over the great headlands. But she did not know where they went after the moon had gone down.

One very bright moonlight night in the early autumn, when the Piskey-stools* were thick on New-train Cliffs, old Jinnie came again to watch the Piskeys; and when she got there, there were not any to be seen. She could not understand it, and she went and looked at the Piskey-stools to see if they

* Mushrooms.

The Piskeys who Carried their Beds

were sitting on any of them having a chat, which they sometimes did when they were tired of dancing; but every Piskey-stool on the cliffs was unoccupied.

As she was wondering what had become of the Piskeys, she heard shrieks of tiny laughter, like the giggles of kittiwakes, coming up from Newtrain Bay under the cliffs; and she hastened down the steep road leading to the bay—which was romantic-looking, and almost shut in by tall cliffs—as fast as her old legs would take her.

When she got to the bottom of the road, she met four little Piskeys coming up, carrying a large Piskey-bag between them; and being very anxious to know what they were going to do with the dark-brown thing, she said:

'My little dears, will you kindly tell me what you are going to do with the Piskey-bag?'

They were evidently too surprised to answer the old woman at once, for she had never spoken to them before, and they stared up at her open-mouthed.

'To sleep in when the cold weather comes,' answered a Piskey at last.

'They are ever so comfortable to snuggle under when the snow is on the ground,' said another little Piskey.

'Sleep in them, do you?' cried old Jinnie, greatly interested. 'To think of it now! I expect they are as warm as the blanketing the blanket-weavers weave in their looms at Padstow. But I never knew before you slept in the bags; I thought you kept your money in them.'

'We don't, then,' cried the Piskeys, grinning all over their little elf faces, which were almost as brown as the Piskey-bag they were carrying. 'We use the tiny young bags to keep our money in, not big ones like this.'

'Up we go!' cried one of the Piskeys to his companions, giving the one nearest him a poke in his ribs; and the four little Brown Men began to ascend the steep road, carrying the Piskey-bag by its four tails, swinging it to and fro, and shrieking with laughter as they swung it.

Jinnie watched them for a few minutes, and then went down to the pebbly beach, where she saw dozens of little Brown Men in companies of four, each company bearing a Piskey-bag between them.

There was a long string of these Little People from the water's edge to where she met them, which was about a dozen yards from the foot of the steep road.

The little Brown Men took no notice of her, and swung the bags just as did the first quartette, seemingly unconscious that she was watching them, and laughed and joked among themselves as they swung them.

Old Jinnie followed them up the beach and road, and she wondered to herself where they were going to take the bags; but she never knew, for when they reached the top of the cliff where they danced, they vanished, Piskey-bags and all!

The Fairy Whirlwind

The Fairy Whirlwind

A YOUNG married woman, who was very pretty, lived with her husband in a sweet little cottage by the sea. The cottage was cob-walled, and had a small flower-garden in its front, which was a picture in the early springtime with periwinkles and gilliflowers, and in the summer-time with roses and hollyhocks. There was another garden belonging to the cottage, but it was only for vegetables, and was on the top of a cliff quite five minutes' walk from the cottage.

This young wife and her husband, who was a waggoner, had one little child a few months old. The child was very dear to them both, and they thought she was the sweetest and most beautiful little baby in all the world. The fairies must have been quite of the same opinion, as you will see.

One afternoon the young wife was about to make an Irish stew for her husband's supper, when she found she had not enough potatoes in the house to make it.

As she took her sun-bonnet from its peg to go up to the cliff garden to dig some up, her baby, who was lying in its wooden cradle, puckered its fair little face and began to cry.

185

North Cornwall Fairies

'I believe the darling knows I am going out,' cried the fond young mother. 'I can't leave her here all by her little self; I must take her with me.' And when she had put on her bonnet and a basket for the potatoes on her arm, she lifted the baby out of the cradle and took her with her to the cliff, fondling the dear little thing and talking to it as she went.

When she had reached the cliff-garden, she stood on the edge of the cliff with her flaxen-haired babe in her arms, looking out over the sea. It was a lovely June day, and the water was as quiet as a mill-pond and blue as vipers' bugloss, she told her baby. 'Just the sort of weather for my pretty to be out in,' she cried, hugging the child.

Mrs. Davies, as the young woman was called, after gazing out over the sea for a few minutes, laid her baby down on the top of a potato ridge, close to where a succory and a knapweed grew side by side, and interlaced their blue and purple blossoms. When the babe had fixed its eyes upon the flowers and cooed to them in baby fashion, she set to work to dig up the potatoes.

She had not been digging very long when she heard a curious noise behind her, like the sound of soft wind in trees, but there were no trees in the cliff-garden, and not wind enough to move even the potato leaves.

She dropped the biddix * to see what it was that made so strange a sound, and as she dropped it she

* A double digging tool—one end pointed, the other flattened.

The Fairy Whirlwind

was caught in a whirlwind—a Fairy Whirlwind, she said it was—which whirled her round and round like a whirligig; and as she whirled she was enveloped in a cloud of fine grey pillum, or dust, and she could not see anything beyond her nose.

When the whirlwind went away—and it vanished as suddenly as it came—she found herself close to the edge of the cliff ever so far away from her baby.

Fearing she knew not what for her child, she ran over to it to see if it was quite safe; and to her horror, there, where her own fair little baby had lain, she saw a dark, wizen little creature, with a face wrinkled all over like an old woman's!

'That is not my little maid,' she shrieked; 'it's a changeling! The wicked Little People envied us our little beauty, and have stolen her away, and left one of their own ugly brats in her place. They raised a Fairy Whirlwind to hide from me what they were doing, the wicked, wicked little things!'

Mrs. Davies never knew how long she stood staring down in hopeless misery upon the ugly babe the Small People had left there on the potato ridge in place of her own; but in the end she took it up in her arms and carried it down to the cottage.

Her husband was at home by this time, wondering what had become of his wife and child, and you might have knocked him down with a straw when she poured out her woe to him, and showed him the ugly dark babe the fairies had exchanged for their own beautiful babe.

North Cornwall Fairies

'What must I do with it?' she asked piteously, when her husband turned away from it with grief in his eyes and sorrow in his heart.

'Keep it till the Small People are tired of our little handsome,' he said, 'and be good to it if you can. If we ain't kind to the fairies' cheeld, they won't be kind to ours, that's certain.'

So the young woman and her husband, for the sake of their own flaxen-haired, blue-eyed little darling the Small People had envied and taken away, were very kind to the babe they had left in its place. They hoped, as they took care of it, although they never loved it, that the fairies would quickly grow tired of their child and bring her back; but they hoped in vain.

A year after the Small People had raised a whirlwind, the fairies' cheeld, as Mrs. Davies and her husband called the babe left on the potato ridge in place of their own, pined away and died; but the little human child with its flaxen curls and eyes of Cornish blue was never seen by mortal eyes after the fairies had stolen it.

Notes

'THE ADVENTURES OF A PISKEY IN SEARCH OF HIS LAUGH.'

THE Piskeys are said to have 'a kind of music,' and to dance to the strains of fairy fiddles.

There are Piskey-rings on many of the Cornish cliffs and headlands. The country people say the Piskeys make them in the night. The rings, anyhow, spring up suddenly like mushrooms!

The legend of the mole is still current in North Cornwall, and its tiny hands are shown as evidence that it was once a very proud and vain lady, who said that the ground was not fit for her dainty feet to walk on. As a punishment for her overwhelming vanity and pride, she was turned into a mole to walk underground.

There is more than one quaint conceit about Jack-o'-the-Lantern or the little Man-o'-the-Lantern. Some say he walks about carrying a lantern, others that he goes over the moors *in* his lantern. He is the Piskey Puck.

There are many weird stories told about Giant Tregeagle. I have given one of the simplest, but only as far as it has to do with North Cornwall. It is said that his shadow still flits over the moorlands in the neighbourhood of Dozmare Pool, and that the pool itself is the Mother of Storms, being moved by supernatural influences.

North Cornwall Fairies

There has always been a tradition that an underground water-way led from Dozmare Pool to the sea, but there is no tradition that Merlin ever came out of the place where the Lady of the Lake put him, or that he was the Bargeman of the moorland lake.

The little fairy riders, or 'night-riders,' as we Cornish call them, are, I believe, peculiar to North and East Cornwall. They do not seem to have been a kind Little People. They never had any consideration for the horses and colts which they took out of farmers' stables near their haunts, but rode them over the moors and commons till they were ready to drop, and then left them to perish or to find their way back to their stables as best they could. They made stirrups out of the colts' manes and tails.

The legend that King Arthur never died is still extant, and it is said that he haunts the dark Tintagel cliffs and the ruins of the old castle where he was born in the form of a red-legged chough.

'LEGEND OF THE PADSTOW DOOMBAR.'

The above legend is doubtless a myth, but it is a fact that a wailing cry is sometimes heard on the Doombar after a fearful gale and loss of life on that fateful bar, like a woman bewailing the dead.

'THE LITTLE CAKE-BIRD.'

In the neighbourhood of St. Columb the children used to be told that when they were in bed and asleep the dear little Piskeys would pass over their noses and order their dreams. One of the strange conceits about the Piskeys was told to me not long ago by a native of Cornwall. He said he had heard the old Granfers and Grannies say that the Piskeys were the spirits of still-born and unbaptized children, which will perhaps explain the curious belief that Small People were not good enough for heaven nor bad enough for hell. The gay little

Notes

Piskeys seem to have their wistful moments and yearnings for higher things. They are said to listen at windows and doors in moorland villages when Christian people are saying their prayers.

It was the custom in some parts of Cornwall to put a piece of dough in the shape of a bird on the top of the children's Christmas Eve buns, to remind the children that the white-winged Angels sang when the Babe of Bethlehem was born. If I remember rightly, the buns were eaten hot from the oven.

'THE IMPOUNDED CROWS.'

This is a well-known legend. The Crow Pound, where little St. Neot impounded the pilfering crows, was in existence not a great while ago. It is now a field.

'THE OLD SKY WOMAN.'

Wherever the snow falls in North Cornwall, especially at Padstow, little children cry one to the other that the Old Woman is up in the sky plucking her goose.

'THE LITTLE HORSES AND HORSEMEN OF PADSTOW.'

The quaint little figures on the housetop in the old town of Padstow are visible to all the passers-by, and sometimes strangers ask why they were put there—a difficult question to answer, as nobody knows for certain. Perhaps they were placed on the ridge of the house for the Piskeys to dance on, or for the fairy riders to ride. Or maybe they were put there in the days of the Civil Wars, as a token that the house on which the little steeds and the little horsemen were perched was a refuge for King Charles' cavaliers. There is no tradition about the small horses and their riders, but the children were always told, as the tale says, that when they heard the clock strike twelve they galloped round the market and town.

North Cornwall Fairies

'THE PISKEYS' REVENGE.'

It used to be held, and is still told, that the Piskeys came in through the keyhole and ate up the good things. Children, when they knew that cakes were made and asked to have some, were told that the Piskeys had eaten them all. They had a special liking for junkets and sugar biscuits.

'THE PISKEYS WHO DID AUNT BETSY'S WORK.'

Some of the Piskeys were kindly disposed, and were credited with doing kindly acts, and it is said that they often came into the cottages in the night-time and cleaned them. When the cottages looked very clean and neat it was said that the Piskeys had done it.

'HOW JAN BREWER WAS PISKEY-LADEN.'

Legends about Piskey-led people are as plentiful as blackberries. The present one comes from the neighbourhood of Constantine.

WELLS GARDNER, DARTON AND CO., LTD., LONDON.

Lightning Source UK Ltd.
Milton Keynes UK
UKOW030752121211

183623UK00006BA/16/P